CompTIA

Network +

Full-length CompTIA Network+ (N10-007) Practice Exams

N10-007

Dennis Cromwell

Table of Contents

Practice Exam #1

QUESTION 1:

(This Performance is a simulated -Based Question. On the real certification exam, you will be asked to drag-and-drop the correct antennas onto the APs.)

Your company has just purchased a new building down the street for its executive suites. You have been asked to select the proper type of antennas to establish a wireless connection between the two buildings.

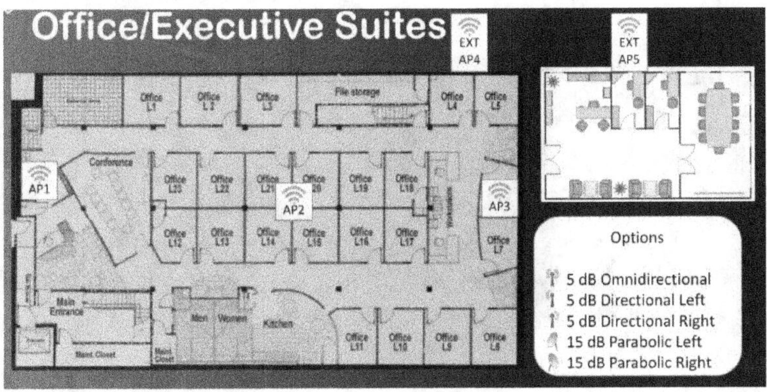

Which of the following is the BEST antenna configuration to use for AP4 and AP5 in order to control the signal propagation and to minimize the chances of the signal being intercepted?

1. Pick a 5 dB Right Directional for AP4 and a 5 dB Left Direction for AP5
2. Pick a 15 dB Right Parabolic for AP4 and a 15 dB Left Parabolic for AP5
3. Pick a 5 dB Left Directional for AP4 and a 5 dB Right Direction for AP5
4. Pick a 15 dB Left Parabolic for AP4 and a 15 dB Right Parabolic for AP5

Correct Answer(s): 2

Explanation:

Parabolic antennas work well for outside wireless applications where you want directional control of the signal (such as when connecting two buildings together)

"

and over longer distance (such as "down the street" as in this scenario). The other possible option was the Directional anntennas, but the signal stength of 5 dB would not be sufficient for an outdoor wireless connection over the distance presented in this scenario.

QUESTION 2:

(This is a simulated Performance-Based Question.)

The company's corporate headquarters provided your branch office a portion of their Class C subnet to use at a new office location. In the next several questions, you will be asked to allocate the minimum number of addresses using CIDR notation in order to accommodate each department's needs.

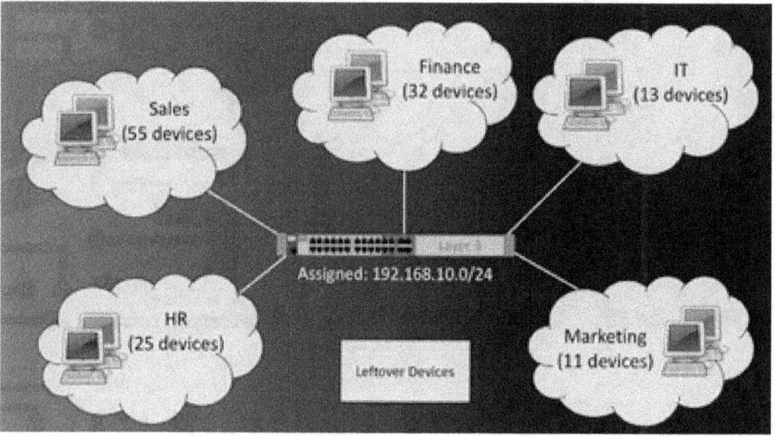

What is the correct CIDR notation for the Sales department's subnet which requires 55 devices?

1. /25
2. /26
3. /27
4. /28
5. /29
6. /30

Correct Answer(s): 2

Explanation:

Since the Sales department needs 55 devices plus a network ID and broadcast IP, it will require 57 IP addresses. The smallest subnet that can fit 57 IPs is a /26 (64 IPs).

QUESTION 3:

(This is a simulated Performance-Based Question.)

Computer to Switch

What type of cable would you use to connect a computer to a switch?

1. Crossover
2. RG-6
3. Rollover
4. RS-232
5. Straight-through

Correct Answer(s): 5

Explanation:

Straight-through cables are used to connect a computer to a hub or switch. If this was a real question on the exam, you would have the words provided in a list, and you would drag them below the appropriate drawing.

QUESTION 4:

(This is a simulated Performance-Based Question.) A home user performs a speed test using SpeedTest.net and receives the follow report:

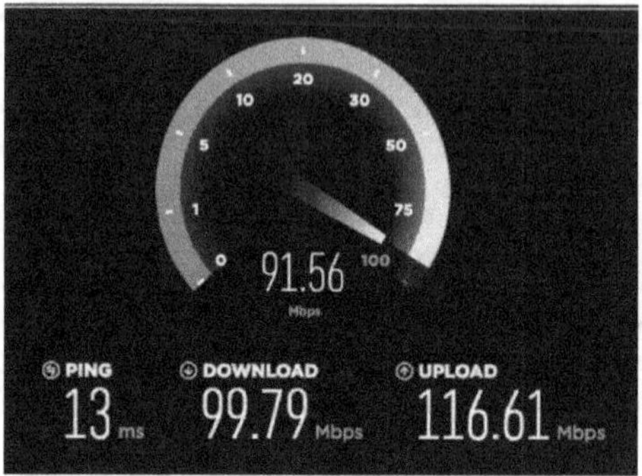

Which of the following is a correct interpretation of these results?

1. The user's PC downloaded 99.79 MB of data from the website and uploaded 116.61 MB of data to the website.
2. The user's PC is downloading information faster than it uploads because it has an asynchronous connection.
3. The user's PC is receiving data at 99.79 Mbps and sending data to the server at 116.61 Mbps.
4. The SpeedTest website is downloading data to its server at 99.79 Mbps and uploading data from its server at 116.61 Mbps.

Correct Answer(s): 3

Explanation:

The user's PC is receiving data at 99.79 Mbps and sending data to the server at 116.61 Mbps. When you run a speed test, your computer downloads a sample file from the test server, then uploads it back to the server to determine your connection speed.

QUESTION 5:

(This is a simulated Performance-Based Question.) You are a network administrator troubleshooting an issue with a newly-installed web server. The web server is available to internal network users, but users from outside the internal network (Internet users) cannot reach the server. You run an IPCONFIG and receive the configuration below:

```
IP:          192.168.0.10
NETMASK:     255.255.254.0
GATEWAY:     192.168.0.2
DNS:         10.10.0.255
```

Which of the following is the MOST LIKELY reason why the server is unreachable from the Internet?

1. The configured DNS server is not reachable by the web server.
2. The gateway IP has been configured incorrectly.
3. The Layer 3 switch port connecting the web server is blocking port 80.
4. NAT has not been configured on the border firewall.

Correct Answer(s): 4

Explanation:

The most likely cause is that the NAT has not been configured on the border firewall properly. This would cause the internal network users to still be able to access the web servers (since internal traffic doesn't have to transit the firewall), but would still prevent the Internet users from accessing the web server.

QUESTION 6:

It is 3 am on a Saturday and you just received a call from a system administrator that reports multiple network outages across the office network. It is snowing heavily outside and the roads are inaccessible for you to get to the building to check the configuration of the network devices. What technology should you use to connect to the network from your home office in order to troubleshoot the network outages?

1. HTTP
2. Telnet
3. SNMP
4. SSH

Correct Answer(s): 4

Explanation:

You should use a VPN or a SSH connection to remotely connect to your office network remotely from home. Either of these options would provide you with an encrypted tunnel to the office network and allow you to begin troubleshooting remotely just as if you were physically located inside the building. SNMP isn't used for troubleshooting, but instead for network monitoring and reporting. Telnet and

HTTP are both insecure and should not be used to connect to your office network from home without the fear of the information being intercepted or changed.

QUESTION 7:

Your company has two office buildings which are connected via copper network cable that is buried underground. There is some construction being performed near the buildings. Now, the second building discovers they have suffered a network outage that doesn't appear to be temporary. What is the MOST likely cause of the outage?

1. Cross-talk on the cable
2. An open circuit has been created
3. Electromagnetic interference on the cable
4. Signal attenuation on the cable

Correct Answer(s): 2

Explanation:

Since the issue started after construction began, it is most likely that the construction crew broke the cable during digging operations. This can cause an open circuit or short circuit, depending on how the cable was cut/broken by the construction workers. This can be verified using a Time-Domain Reflectometer to determine exactly where in the cable the break has occurred.

QUESTION 8:

Mark is setting up a DHCP server on a segment of the corporate LAN. Which of the following options is NOT required in the DHCP scope in order to allow hosts on that LAN segment to be assigned a dynamic IP addresses and to still be able to access the Internet and internal company servers?

1. Default gateway
2. Reservations
3. DNS servers
4. Subnet mask

Correct Answer(s): 2

Explanation:

In order to effectively access the Internet, the DHCP must provide a default gateway, DNS server, and subnet mask to each client. Using DHCP reservations is not required to be configured to meet the requirements provided in the question.

QUESTION 9:

A technician added memory to a router, but that memory is never recognized by the router. The router is then powered down, and the technician relocates all of the memory to different modules. On startup, the router does not boot and displays memory errors. Which of the following is the MOST likely cause of this issue?

1. VTP
2. Driver update
3. ESD
4. Halon particles

Correct Answer(s): 3

Explanation:

The most likely cause is that the memory chips are bad, because they have suffered from electrostatic discharge (ESD) during the installation and movement of the chips. (This question references a concept covered in-depth in your A+ curriculum, but is considered fair game on the Network+ exam.)

QUESTION 10:

A company owns four kiosks that are in close proximity within a shopping center. The owner is concerned about someone accessing the Internet via the kiosk's wireless network. What should be implemented to provide wireless access only to the employees working at the kiosk?

1. Firewall
2. Web filtering
3. MAC filtering
4. Host-based antivirus

Correct Answer(s): 3

Explanation:

MAC Filtering will control access to the network by restricting access to only certain devices.

QUESTION 11:

A technician has installed an 802.11n network and most users are able to see speeds of up to 300Mbps. There are few users who have an 802.11n network card but are unable to get speeds higher than 108Mbps. What should the technician do to fix the issue?

1. Upgrade the OS version to 64-bit
2. Roll back the firmware on WLAN card
3. Install a vulnerability patch
4. Upgrade the WLAN card driver

Correct Answer(s): 4

Explanation:

Wireless N networks can support up to 600Mbps with the proper software drivers for the network cards. Without them, they can only achieve 108Mbps since they cannot communicate with the increased data compression rates.

QUESTION 12:

A malicious user is blocking mobile devices from connecting to the Internet when other people are in the coffee shop. What is the malicious user implementing?

Removing the AP from the classroom

1. ACL
2. Jamming
3. Firewall
4. IPS

Correct Answer(s): 2

Explanation:

Jamming is one of the many exploits used to compromise a wireless environment. It works by denying service to authorized users as legitimate traffic is jammed by the overwhelming frequencies of illegitimate traffic.

QUESTION 13:

Which of the following provides origin authenticity through source authentication, data integrity through hash functions, and confidentiality through encryption protection for IP packets?

1. IPSEC
2. SHA
3. DES
4. CRC

Correct Answer(s): 1

Explanation:

Internet Protocol Security (IPSec) is a network protocol that encrypts and authenticates data sent over a network. All other choices offer encryption or authentication.

QUESTION 14:

Routing prefixes, which are assigned in blocks by IANA and distributed by the Regional Internet Registry (RIR), are known as what?

1. Network handle
2. Autonomous system number
3. Route aggregation
4. Top level domain

Correct Answer(s): 2

Explanation:

ASN (or Autonomous System Number) are used to control routing with BGP routing protocols to route traffic across the network.

QUESTION 15:

Which of the following BEST describes how a DHCP reservation works?

1. By leasing a set of reserved IP addresses according to their category
2. By letting the network switches assign IP addresses from a reserved pool
3. By assigning options to the computers on the network by priority
4. By matching a MAC address to an IP address within the DHCP scope

Correct Answer(s): 4

Explanation:

When the client requests an IP address by sending a message on the network to the DHCP server, the DHCP server will assign an IP from its DHCP scope to the client and reserve it based on the client's MAC address.

QUESTION 16:

Which of the following is used to proxy client requests for IP configurations across different network segments?

1. DHCP relay
2. SOCKS
3. Teredo tunneling
4. Reverse proxy

Correct Answer(s): 1

Explanation:

A DHCP client is an Internet host using DHCP to obtain configuration parameters such as an IP address. A DHCP relay agent is any host that forwards DHCP packets between clients and servers. Relay agents are used to forward requests and replies between clients and servers when they are not on the same physical subnet.

QUESTION 17:

A technician installs a new WAP and users in the area begin to report poor performance. The technician uses a ping and only 3 of the 5 packets respond. When the technician tests the connection from a wired connection, it responds with 5 of 5 packets. What tool should the network technician use next?

1. Port scanner tool
2. Interface monitoring tool
3. Packet capture tool
4. Spectrum Analyzer tool

Correct Answer(s): 4

Explanation:

A spectrum analyzer is a device that displays signal amplitude (strength) as it varies by signal frequency. Since the issue only occurs when connecting wirelessly, it is most like a spectrum interference issue.

QUESTION 18:

A network technician is connecting three temporary office trailers with a point-to-multipoint microwave radio solution in a wooded area. The microwave radios are up and the network technician can ping devices in all office trailers, however, connectivity is sporadic. What is the cause of this issue?

1. Latency
2. Throttling
3. Interference
4. Split horizon

Correct Answer(s): 3

Explanation:

As a process of elimination, throttling slows down speed and latency slows down speed even further. Split horizon prevents loops so it only makes sense that interference is the choice. Also, interference causes drops in connections in many circumstances.

QUESTION 19:

You are troubleshooting the network connectivity between a remote server and your workstation. Which of the following tools should you use to determine the connection path between your workstation and the remote server?

1. pathping
2. tcpdump
3. netstat
4. ping

Correct Answer(s): 1

Explanation:

Pathping works on Windows systems from the command line. This command provides details of the path between two hosts and Ping-like statistics for each node in the path based on samples taken over a time period, depending on how many nodes are between the start and end host. The advantages of PathPing over ping and traceroute are that each node is pinged as the result of a single command, and that the behavior of nodes is studied over an extended time period, rather than the default ping sample of four messages or default traceroute single route trace. The disadvantage is that it takes a total of 25 seconds per hop to show the ping statistics. This makes pathping the best option to use.

QUESTION 20:

In what type of attack does the potential intruder trick a user into providing sensitive information?

1. Social engineering
2. Bluesnarfing

3. Man-in-the-middle
4. Evil Twin

Correct Answer(s): 1

Explanation:

Social engineering is the art of convincing people to reveal confidential information to the intruder.

QUESTION 21:

Which of the following network protocols is used to send email from one server to another server?

1. RTP
2. SNMP
3. POP
4. SMTP

Correct Answer(s): 4

Explanation:

Simple Mail Transfer Protocol (SMTP) is a well-known application that uses port 25 for sending email from one server to another server.

QUESTION 22:

A network administrator is tasked with building a wireless network in a new building located right next door. The wireless clients should not have visibility to one another but should have visibility to the wired users. Users must seamlessly migrate between the buildings while maintaining a constant connection to the LAN. How should he configure the new wireless network in the new building?

1. Use the same SSIDs on different channels and AP isolation
2. Use different SSIDs on different channels and VLANs
3. Use different SSIDs on the same channels with VLANs
4. Use the same SSIDs on same channels with AP isolation

Correct Answer(s): 1

Explanation:

For users to be able to seamlessly migrate between the two buildings, both Access Points (AP) must use the same SSIDs. They must be on different channels though.

Otherwise, interference would occur. Access Point (AP) isolation is a technique for preventing mobile devices connected to an AP from communicating directly with each other.

QUESTION 23:

At which of the following OSI layer does QoS operate?

1. Layer 1
2. Layer 3
3. Layer 5
4. Layer 7

Correct Answer(s): 2

Explanation:

Quality of Service (QoS) occurs at both Layer 2 and Layer 3 of the OSI Model.

QUESTION 24:

You are trying to connect to a router using SSH to check its configuration. Your attempts to connect to the device over SSH keep failing. You ask another technician to verify that SSH is properly configured, enabled on the router, and is allowing access from all subnets. She attempts to connect to the router over SSH from her workstation and confirms all the settings are correct. Which of the following steps might you have missed in setting up your SSH client that is preventing you from connecting to the router?

1. Change default credentials
2. Perform file hashing
3. Generate a new SSH key
4. Update firmware

Correct Answer(s): 3

Explanation:

When configuring your SSH connection, you must ensure that a key is established between your client and the server. If you never setup an SSH key, you will need to generate a new key to get SSH to connect properly. Since the other technician was able to connect on her machine, we can rule out a SSH server issue, so it must be an issue with your account or client. The only option that relates solely to your account or client is the possibility that a key was not generated.

QUESTION 25:

Your network relies on the use of ATM cells. At which layer of the OSI model do
ATM cells operate?

1. Network
2. Session
3. Transport
4. Data link

Correct Answer(s): 4

Explanation:

In the data link layer (layer 2) of the OSI model, the basic unit of transfer is called a
frame. In an ATM network, these frames are called cells and are of a fixed (53 octets
or bytes) length that allows for faster switching of the cells across the network.

QUESTION 26:

A technician is concerned about security and is asked to set up a network
management protocol. Which network management protocol will provide the best
security?

1. SLIP
2. SNMPv3
3. TKIP
4. SNMPv2

Correct Answer(s): 2

Explanation:

Simple Network Management Protocol (SNMP) is an Internet-standard protocol for
collecting and organizing information about managed devices on IP networks and for
modifying that information to change device behavior. Three significant versions of
SNMP have been created, with SNMPv3 being the most secure.

QUESTION 27:

The UPS that provides backup power to your server is malfunctioning because its
internal battery has died. To replace the battery, you must shut down the server,
unplug it from the UPS, and unplug the UPS from its power source (the wall outlet).
You perform these actions but think that there has to be a better way to increase the
availability of the server in the future. Which of the following recommendations

would BEST increase the availability of the server based on your experience with the
UPS battery replacement?

1. Install a second UPS in the rack
2. Install a surge protector instead
3. Add a redundant power supply to the server
4. Replace the UPS with a generator

Correct Answer(s): 3

Explanation:

The BEST recommendation would be to install a redundant power supply in the
server. Adding a second UPS would not solve the problem if the server still only has
one power supply available. Switching from a UPS to a generator will not solve this
issue, either, because generators also requirement scheduled maintenance and
downtimes. Finally, adding a surge protector won't provide power when you need to
power off a UPS for a battery replacement.

QUESTION 28:

What tool would a network technician use to troubleshoot a span of single-mode
fiber cable?

1. Punchdown tool
2. Spectrum analyzer
3. Ethernet tester
4. OTDR

Correct Answer(s): 4

Explanation:

The other answers are used with copper cables (like CAT5). An optical time-domain
reflectometer (OTDR) is an optoelectronic instrument used to characterize an optical
fiber. An OTDR is the optical equivalent of an electronic time domain reflectometer.

QUESTION 29:

An offsite backup service is involved in an investigation currently. Because of this,
they are not recycling the outdated tapes. Which of the following is the MOST likely
reason for this?

1. The process of discovery
2. A chain of custody breach
3. A data transport request

4. A notice of a legal hold

Correct Answer(s): 4

Explanation:

A legal hold is a process that an organization uses to preserve all forms of relevant information when litigation is reasonably anticipated. If a legal hold notice has been given to the backup service, they will not destroy the old backup tapes until the hold is lifted.

QUESTION 30:

Your company has decided to upgrade its legacy phone system to use VoIP devices instead. The new phones will download the configurations from a server each time they boot up. Which of the following ports needs to be opened on the firewall to ensure the phones can communicate with the TFTP server?

1. 21
2. 53
3. 69
4. 161

Correct Answer(s): 3

Explanation:

TFTP uses port 69 to communicate.

QUESTION 31:

Which of the following network concepts is prevented by using a split horizon?

1. Large routing tables
2. Duplicate addresses
3. Collisions
4. Loops

Correct Answer(s): 4

Explanation:

In computer networking, split-horizon route advertisement is a method of preventing routing loops in distance-vector routing protocols by prohibiting a router from advertising a route back onto the interface from which it was learned.

QUESTION 32:

Susan is a network administrator who is in the process of preparing and cleaning network switches for resale. She splashes the cleaning agent in her eye and needs to know the procedure to do in order to cleanse her eye. Where should she look to find the right procedure?

1. EULA
2. MSDS
3. SLA
4. MOU

Correct Answer(s): 2

Explanation:

The Manufacturers Safety Data Sheet (MSDS) lists the chemical composition of the solution and states the relevant protocol for first aid treatment. (This is another concept covered by the A+ exam, but if you didn't know it, you should have been able to guess it based on eliminating the other 3 options.

QUESTION 33:

When installing a network cable with multiple strands, a network technician pulled the cable past a sharp edge and exposes the copper conductor on several of the wire strands. These exposed wires come into contact with each other forming an electrical connection. Which of the following conditions was created?

1. Short
2. Open
3. Electrostatic discharge
4. Crosstalk

Correct Answer(s): 1

Explanation:

A short in electrical terms is an abbreviation for a short circuit. This generally means that there is an unintended connection between two points allowing current to flow where it should not. In your particular case, it means that a cable is damaged and that two or more of the conductors are connected together causing the cable to fail.

QUESTION 34:

Which of the following applies to data as it travels from Layer 1 to Layer 7 of the OSI model?

1. Tagging
2. Encapsulation
3. Tunneling
4. De-encapsulation

Correct Answer(s): 4

Explanation:

De-encapsulation occurs as the data travels up the OSI layers. As information travels down the OSI model from layer 7 to layer 1, it is encapsulated along the way.

QUESTION 35:

A network administrator was told by the Chief Information Officer (CIO) to set up a new office with a network that has redundancy. What topology would BEST meet the CIO's requirement?

1. Hybrid
2. Bus
3. Mesh
4. Star

Correct Answer(s): 3

Explanation:

A mesh topology connects every endpoint to every other endpoint, creating a fully redundant network.

QUESTION 36:

An administrator arrives at work and is told that network users are unable to access the file server. The administrator logs into the server and sees the updates were automatically installed last night and the network connection shows "limited" with no availability. What rollback action should the technician perform?

1. Browser on the server
2. Server's NIC drivers
3. Server's IP address
4. Antivirus updates

Correct Answer(s): 2

Explanation:

An IP address is attached to a NIC's MAC address, which would not change in the event of an update. Sometimes, software updates can adjust hardware driver settings accidentally, so it is a good practice to always review these settings first to eliminate this.

QUESTION 37:

Jason is the network manager and is leading a project to deploy a SAN. He is working with the vendor's support technician to properly set up and configure the SAN on the network. To begin SAN I/O optimization, what should Jason need to provide to the vendor support technician?

1. Network diagrams
2. Baseline documents
3. Asset management document
4. Access to the data center

Correct Answer(s): 1

Explanation:

A network diagram is a visual representation of network architecture. It maps out the structure of a network with a variety of different symbols and line connections. This information will be important when deploying a Storage Area Network (SAN).

QUESTION 38:

You are working as a service desk analyst. This morning, you have received multiple calls from users reporting that they cannot access websites from their work computers. You decide to troubleshoot the issue by opening up your command prompt on your Windows machine and running a program to determine where the network connectivity outage is occurring. Which tool should you use to determine if the issue is on the intranet portion of your corporate network or if the issue is occurring due to a problem with your ISP?

1. netstat
2. nslookup
3. ping
4. tracert

Correct Answer(s): 4

Explanation:

Tracert is a command-line utility that is used to trace the path of an IP packet as it moves from its source to its destination. While using ping will tell you if the remote website is reachable or not, it will not tell you where the connection is broken. Tracert, though, performs a series of ICMP echo requests to determine which device in the connection path is not responding appropriately. This will help to identify if the connectivity issue lies within your intranet or is a problem with the ISPs connection.

QUESTION 39:

What happens when convergence on a routed network occurs?

1. All routers are using hop count as the metric
2. All routers have the same routing table
3. All routers learn the route to all connected networks
4. All routers use route summarization

Correct Answer(s): 3

Explanation:

Routers exchange routing topology information with each other by using a routing protocol. When all routers have exchanged routing information with all other routers within a network, the routers are said to have converged. In other words: In a converged network, all routers "agree" on what the network topology looks like.

QUESTION 40:

The accounting department has been relocated to a new area of the building which is more than 70 meters away from the closest IDF. In order to comply with a SLA which requires that 10Gb speeds be provided, what type of media should be installed?

1. CAT6a
2. CAT5e
3. 802.11n
4. 802.11ac

Correct Answer(s): 1

Explanation:

Cat6a is the only one listed that can meet 10 Gbps. CAT5e and 802.11 ac can only support speeds up to 1 Gbps.

QUESTION 41:

A network administrator receives a call asking for assistance with connecting to the network. The person on the phone asks for the IP address, subnet mask, and VLAN required to access the network. What type of attack might this be?

1. Social engineering
2. Spoofing
3. Zero-day attack
4. VLAN hopping

Correct Answer(s): 1

Explanation:

Social engineering is a type of attack on a network using confidence and gullibility of users to gain access. It is the only type of attack on a network that is directed towards the human element. The human interaction with the network administrator makes the other three answers incorrect.

QUESTION 42:

What would be used in an IP-based video conferencing deployment?

1. RS-232
2. 56k modem
3. Bluetooth
4. Codec

Correct Answer(s): 4

Explanation:

The term "codec" is a concatenation of "encoder" and "decoder". In video conferencing, a codec is a software (or can be a hardware) that compresses (encodes) raw video data before it is transmitted over a network. Generally, audio/video conferencing systems utilize the H.323 protocol with various codecs like H.263 and H.264 to operate.

QUESTION 43:

A network administrator is assigned an approved change request with a change window of 120 minutes. After 90 minutes, the change is stuck on step five of a five-step change. The network manager decides to initiate a rollback. Which describes what the network administrator should do next?

1. Return the system to step four since this was the last working step
2. Request additional time since the change is near completion
3. Leave the change as is and inform users of a workaround
4. Return the system back to the original state before the change

Correct Answer(s): 4

Explanation:

By performing a rollback, the administrator will change everything back to the last known good configuration prior to the change being started.

QUESTION 44:

A technician is called to investigate a connectivity issue to a remote office that is connected by fiber optic cable. Using a light meter, it is determined that the dB loss is excessive. The installation has been working for several years. The switch was recently moved to the other side of the room and a new patch cable installed. Which of the following is most likely the reason for this problem?

1. Distance limitations
2. Wavelength mismatch
3. Bend radius limitation
4. Dirty connectors

Correct Answer(s): 4

Explanation:

When Fiber Optic Connectors become dirty, the loss of signal can cause severe problems and performance issues. The technician will need to use appropriate cleaning cloth to clean the dirty connectors and restore the service.

QUESTION 45:

A user is unable to connect to a server in another building and discovers the following while troubleshooting the issue:

1) Client PC 1 has an IP address if 172.16.10.25/25

2) PC 1 can successfully ping its gateway of 172.16.10.1/25, which is an interface of
router A

3) Server A is named "BLDGRILFESVR01' and has an IP address of
172.16.10.145/25

4) PC 2 with an IP address of 172.16.10.200/25 can successfully ping server A

However, when PC 1 pings Server A, it gets an error of destination host unreachable.
Which of the following might be the issue?

1. Link from SERVER A to PC 1 are on different subnets
2. Link from ROUTER A to SERVER A is down
3. Link from PC 1 to ROUTER A has duplex issues
4. Link from SERVER A to PC 2 is down

Correct Answer(s): 1

Explanation:

Since the IPs listed are all using /25 for their CIDR notation, we can determine that
they are on two separate subnets (172.16.10.0-172.16.10.127 and 172.16.10.128-
172.16.10.255).

QUESTION 46:

An organization requires a second technician to verify changes before applying them
to network devices. When checking the configuration of a network device, a
technician determines that a coworker has improperly configured the AS number on
the device. Which of the following might be the result of this?

1. The OSPF not-so-stubby area is misconfigured
2. Reduced wireless network coverage
3. Spanning tree ports in flooding mode
4. BGP routing issues

Correct Answer(s): 4

Explanation:

BGP (Border Gateway Protocol) is used to route data between autonomous systems
(AS). A collection of networks that fall within the same administrative domain is
called an autonomous system (AS). The routers within an AS use an interior gateway
protocol, such as the Routing Information Protocol (RIP) or the Open Shortest Path
First (OSPF) protocol, to exchange routing information among themselves.

QUESTION 47:

An administrator is upgrading the switches in the server room to support 10 Gbps of throughput. The switch will need to take advantage of the existing CAT6a lines that run to each server. Which of the following Ethernet standards should be used to meet this requirement?

1. 10GBaseT
2. 10GBaseFX
3. 10GBaseSR
4. 10GBaseSW

Correct Answer(s): 1

Explanation:

CAT6a can reach speeds of 10 Gbps over 10GBaseT cables. The other cables listed are all fiber cables, and not CAT6a.

QUESTION 48:

While troubleshooting, a technician notices that some clients using FTP still work and that pings to the local routers and servers are working. The technician tries to ping all known nodes on the network and they reply positively, except for one of the servers. The technician notices that ping works only when the host name is used but not when FQDN is used. What server is MOST likely offline?

1. WINS server
2. Domain controller
3. DHCP server
4. DNS server

Correct Answer(s): 4

Explanation:

The DNS Server translates Fully Qualified Domain Names (FQDN) to IP addresses.

QUESTION 49:

Your physical security manager, Janice, wants to ensure she can detect any unauthorized access to the datacenter. Which technology should be used to meet her requirement?

1. Smart card
2. Biometric access

3. Video surveillance
4. Access badge reader

Correct Answer(s): 3

Explanation:

Since her requirement is to detect unauthorized access, video surveillance should be utilized. If she were trying to prevent access from occurring, the other three options would be able to provide that, but they cannot detect unauthorized access (for example, if the attacker stole a valid smart card or access badge).

QUESTION 50:

Which of the following is a logical host on the network where unauthorized users are placed in which they still believe they're on the production network?

1. Virtual server
2. VLAN
3. Honeypot
4. Virtual Terminal

Correct Answer(s): 3

Explanation:

A honeypot is a computer security mechanism set to detect, deflect, or in some manner counteract attempts of unauthorized use of information systems. It acts as a decoy so that hackers think there on the production network, but they're actually not.

QUESTION 51:

You have been asked to create a network where visitors can access the Internet without disrupting the office's own intranet. Which of the following types of networks should you created?

1. Guest network
2. VLAN network
3. Security network
4. DMZ network

Correct Answer(s): 1

Explanation:

Guest network allows anyone to have access to the Internet without having the rights to disrupt the intranet. This network should be logically isolated from the corporate intranet of the office. Generally, these guest networks will provide a direct connection out to the internet with little or no security or monitoring on that network.

QUESTION 52:

An outside organization has completed a penetration test for a company. One of the items on the report is reflecting the ability to read SSL traffic from the web server. What is the MOST likely mitigation for this reported item?

1. Ensure patches are deployed
2. Install an IDS on the network
3. Configure the firewall to block traffic on port 443
4. Implement a VPN for employees

Correct Answer(s): 1

Explanation:

A patch is designed to correct a known bug or fix a known vulnerability, such as in this case to be able to read SSL traffic, in a piece of software.

QUESTION 53:

A network technician is working with a junior technician when the network technician is called away for a more urgent issue. The junior technician orders an SC 80/125 fiber cable instead of an ST 80/125. Which of the following will MOST likely be an issue with the new cable?

1. Wavelength mismatch
2. Distance limitations
3. Connector mismatch
4. Attenuation/DB loss

Correct Answer(s): 3

Explanation:

While both SC and ST are fiber cables, they utilize different connectors. The cable ordered will not be compatible with the current equipment in use.

QUESTION 54:

Which of the following is a document that is used in cyber forensics that lists everywhere evidence has been?

1. Warrant
2. Legal document
3. Chain of custody
4. Forensic report

Correct Answer(s): 3

Explanation:

Chain of custody refers to documentation that identifies all changes in the control, handling, possession, ownership, or custody of a piece of evidence.

QUESTION 55:

A company has just installed a VoIP system on their network. Prior to the installation, all of the switches were upgraded to layer 3 capable in order to more adequately route packets. What network segmentation technique is this an example of?

1. Compliance implementation
2. Separate public/private networking
3. Honeypot implementation
4. Performance optimization

Correct Answer(s): 4

Explanation:

Voice over Internet Protocol (VoIP) performance optimization can help a business improve the quality of its video and audio communications over the Internet by tending to such issues as transport and protocol conversion, as well as mitigation.

QUESTION 56:

A network technician needs to connect two switches. The technician needs a link between them that is capable of handling 10 Gbps of throughput. Which of the following media would BEST meet this requirement?

1. CAT5e cable
2. Coax cable
3. Fiber Optic cable

4. CAT3 cable

Correct Answer(s): 3

Explanation:

To achieve 10 Gbps, you should use CAT 6a or a fiber cable. Since CAT6a isn't an option, fiber is the best answer here. CAT 5e can only operate up to 100 meters at 1 Gbps of speed.

QUESTION 57:

What is an example of a signaling protocol used in VoIP telephony?

1. VRRP
2. H.323
3. RTSP
4. SIP

Correct Answer(s): 4

Explanation:

SIP is the Session Initiation Protocol and it is used for VoIP and audio/video conferencing. Alternatively, you could use the process of elimination to find the correct answer. VRRP is the (virtual router redundancy protocol) that automatically assigns IP routers to hosts, H 323 is something that works with A/V (audio visual), RTSP is a real time streaming protocol designed to control media servers, and SIP is a session initiation protocol. SIP is a signaling protocol used on the application layer.

QUESTION 58:

What is considered a classless routing protocol?

1. IGRP
2. IS-IS
3. RIPv1
4. STP

Correct Answer(s): 2

Explanation:

IS-IS is known as a classless protocol. Classless routing protocols are those protocols that include the subnet mask information when the routing tables or updates are exchanged. Other classless routing protocols include EIGRP, RIPv2 (or newer), and OSPF.

QUESTION 59:

An administrator reassigns a laptop to a different user in the company. Upon delivering the laptop to the new user, the administrator documents the new location, the user of the device, and when the device was reassigned. Which of the following BEST describes these actions?

1. Network map
2. Asset management
3. Change management
4. Baselines

Correct Answer(s): 2

Explanation:

Documenting the location, the user of the device, and the date of the reassignment would be part of the asset management process.

QUESTION 60:

A company is having a new T1 line installed. Which of the following does this connection MOST likely terminate to?

1. Firewall
2. MDF
3. Ethernet router
4. IDF

Correct Answer(s): 2

Explanation:

The telecom company usually terminates the circuits at the Main Distribution Facility (MDF).

QUESTION 61:

A network technician wants to allow HTTP traffic through a stateless firewall. The company uses the 192.168.0.0/24 network. Which of the following ACLs should the technician implement?

1. PERMIT SRCIP 192.168.0.0/24 SPORT:80 DSTIP:192.168.0.0/24 DPORT:80
2. PERMIT SRCIP 192.168.0.0/24 SPORT: ANY DSTIP:ANY DPORT 80
3. PERMIT SRCIP:ANY SPORT:80 DSTIP:192.168.0.0/24 DPORT ANY
4. PERMIT SRCIP: ANYSPORT:80 DSTIP:192.168.0.0/24 DPORT:80

Correct Answer(s): 2

Explanation:

This will permit traffic from the internal network (192.168.0.0/24) from any port to access the external network (any IP) to port 80 (HTTP).

QUESTION 62:

Tim is a network administrator who is setting up three additional switches in his test lab. While configuring the switches, he is verifying the connectivity but finds that when he pings one of the switches using its IP address, he receives "Destination Unreachable". What kind of issue is this?

1. Denial of service attack
2. Misconfigured DNS settings
3. Misconfigured Split Horizon
4. RADIUS authentication errors

Correct Answer(s): 3

Explanation:

Split horizon is a method of preventing a routing loop in a network. If it is misconfigured, the switches would be unable to communicate with each other. None of the other answers provided would prevent communication between the switches.

QUESTION 63:

Which of the following protocols must be implemented in order for two switches to share VLAN information?

1. VTP
2. MPLS
3. STP
4. PPTP

Correct Answer(s): 1

Explanation:

The VLAN Trunking Protocol (VTP) allows a VLAN created on one switch to be propagated to other switches in a group of switches (that is, a VTP domain).

QUESTION 64:

A network technician has just run a new point-to-point fiber link between two local routers. After the fiber has been plugged in on both ends, the interface will not come up. The network technician has double-checked the interface configuration on both routers, both SFPs have been hard-looped to confirm they are functioning, connectors on both ends of the links have been cleaned, and there is sufficient power. What is the cause of the problem?

1. Wavelength mismatch
2. Duplex mismatch
3. Distance limitations
4. Wrong IP address

Correct Answer(s): 1

Explanation:

Wavelength mismatch is when two different transmitters at each end of the cable have either longer or shorter wavelengths. Both transmitters have to be identical on each end of the cable.

QUESTION 65:

Which media access control technology will listen to a cable to ensure there is no traffic being transmitted before sending its traffic, but will implement a back-off timer if a collision does occur?

1. CSMA/CA
2. CSMA/CD
3. Token
4. Demand priority

Correct Answer(s): 2

Explanation:

In networking technologies that use CSMA/CD as their access method, a device first listens to the network media to make sure there is no signal already present from another device before it tries to place its own signal on the media. If a carrier signal is detected on the media, which indicates that a device is currently transmitting a signal, no other device can initiate a transmission until the carrier stops. If no carrier is detected, any device can transmit a signal. If two devices listen to the wire and detect no carrier signal, they may both decide to send signals simultaneously. If this happens, a collision occurs between the two signals generated. Next, both devices detect the collision and stop transmitting their signals immediately, sending out a jamming signal that informs all other devices on the network that a collision has occurred and that they should not transmit. Meanwhile, the two devices whose signals created the collision cease transmitting and wait random intervals of time (usually a few milliseconds) before attempting to retransmit.

QUESTION 66:

Which of the following network infrastructure implementations would be used to connect two remote sales machines back to the main campus for all of their data and voice network traffic?

1. Crossover cable
2. Single mode fiber
3. Satellite
4. MPLS

Correct Answer(s): 2

Explanation:

A crossover cable has a maximum distance of 300 ft over Cat5e. A satellite connection work for line of sight between the office and the satellite, but the signal isn't always reliable or fast enough. MPLS is based on a short path rather than a long path. Single mode fiber can carry different types of data signals over long distances without losing any integrity, therefore it is the best choice. You can lease a pair of single mode fibers from the local telecommunications provider (called dark fiber) since it will already be buried underground and ready for your use.

QUESTION 67:

Which of the following threats can policies, procedures, and end-user training help to effectively mitigate?

1. Zero-day attacks
2. Attempted DDoS attacks
3. Man-in-the-middle attacks
4. Social engineering attempts

Correct Answer(s): 4

Explanation:

Social engineering attempts occur when someone uses something like: phishing (they are attempting to receive your personal information and look legitimate), pretexting (basically they give you a scenario and expect you to react quickly), tailgating (following too closely into a door they aren't allowed in), and many other situations. Proper policies, procedures, and educating your users on the dangers posed by social engineering could prevent them from becoming a victim of a phishing attack, as well as many other attacks.

QUESTION 68:

Your company has just gotten a new OC-12 installed to support your server room. The telecommunications provider has installed the connection from their main offices to your demarcation point. When the installers test the connection from the provider's offices to your demarcation point, everything works properly. You connect the OC-12 to your network, but you are noticing a large amount of dropped packets and errors. You suspect this may be a layer 1 issue. Which of the following should you attempt FIRST to identify the source of the issue?

1. Determine if any devices may be causing EMI on the cable
2. Use a pinout tester to validate the cable's integrity
3. Use an OTDR to validate the cable's integrity
4. Use a multimeter to validate the cable's integrity

Correct Answer(s): 3

Explanation:

You may not know all the details involved in this question, but that is ok. Start with what you do know. The question talks about an OC12 connection. What kind of cable is used with that? An OC-12 is a fiber optic cable. Based on that, you know the only one of these options that has anything to do with a fiber cable is a OTDR (Optical Time-Domain Reflectometer). The other options are all applicable only to copper cables (like Cat 5e, Cat 6a, and T-1).

QUESTION 69:

You are working as a network administrator and are worried about the possibility of an insider threat. You want to enable a security feature that would remember the Layer 2 address that is first connected to a particular switch port in order to prevent someone from unplugging a workstation from the switch port and connecting their own laptop to that same switch port. Which of the following security features would BEST accomplish this goal?

1. NAC
2. Sticky MAC
3. 802.1x
4. ACL

Correct Answer(s): 2

Explanation:

Persistent MAC learning, also known as Sticky MAC, is a port security feature that enables an interface to retain dynamically learned MAC addresses when the switch is restarted or if the interface goes down and is brought back online. This is a security feature that can be used to prevent someone from unplugging their office computer and connecting their own laptop to the network jack without permission, since the switch port connected to that network jack would only allow the computer with the original MAC address to gain connectivity using Sticky MAC.

QUESTION 70:

When a criminal or government investigation is underway, what describes the identification, recovery, or exchange of electronic information relevant to that investigation?

1. Data transport
2. First responder
3. eDiscovery
4. Encryption

Correct Answer(s): 3

Explanation:

Process of elimination: Data transport is the transport of data while the First responder is the "first responder" and encryption is a method of putting data into a tunnel so it's completely secure. That leaves us with eDiscovery. eDiscovery is the term that refers to the process of evidence collection through digital forensics.

QUESTION 71:

You have been asked to install a media converter that connects a newly-installed multimode cable to an existing CAT5e infrastructure. Which type of media converter should you use?

1. Ethernet to coaxial
2. Fiber to Ethernet
3. Fiber to coaxial
4. Multimode to single mode

Correct Answer(s): 2

Explanation:

A media converter is a layer 1 device that changes one type of physical network connection to another. In this case, we are converting multimode (fiber) cable to CAT5e (ethernet) cable.

QUESTION 72:

A project manager is tasked with the planning of a new network installation. The customer requires that everything discussed in the meetings will be installed and configured when a network engineer arrives onsite. Which document should the project manager provide the customer?

1. Acceptable Use Policy
2. Service Level Agreement
3. Statement of Work
4. Security Policy

Correct Answer(s): 3

Explanation:

A Statement of work (SOW) is a document that outlines all the work that is to be performed, as well as the agreed-upon deliverables and timelines.

QUESTION 73:

A network engineer is designing a campus-wide wireless network. Wireless access points will be distributed across the campus for maximum availability. The network is to be designed to handle a large number of roaming wireless devices. What feature should he employ?

1. VLAN pooling
2. Subnetting
3. WPA2
4. LWAPP

Correct Answer(s): 4

Explanation:

LWAPP is the best choice because it serves as a standard single point that allows quick and efficient management of multiple wireless devices at a time.

QUESTION 74:

Which protocol is used to establish a secure and encrypted VPN tunnel that can be initiated through a web browser?

1. PPP
2. PPTP
3. SSL
4. IPSec

Correct Answer(s): 3

Explanation:

An SSL VPN is a type of virtual private network that uses the Secure Sockets Layer protocol in a standard web browser to provide secure, remote-access VPN capability. In modern browsers and servers, it is more common to use TLS (transport layer security) which is the successor to SSL.

QUESTION 75:

What Ethernet feature will allow increased FCoE network throughput as long as all network devices recognize its specific size?

1. Frame relay
2. TCP offloading
3. Jumbo frame
4. Quality of service

Correct Answer(s): 3

Explanation:

By allowing jumbo frames, network throughput can be increased.

Practice Exam #2

QUESTION 1:

(This is a simulated Performance-Based Question. On the real certification exam, you would be asked to drag-and-drop the correct encryption onto the APs.)

Your company has purchased a new building down the street for its executive suites. You have been asked to choose the best encryption for AP4 and AP5 in order to establish a secure wireless connection between the main building and the executive suites.

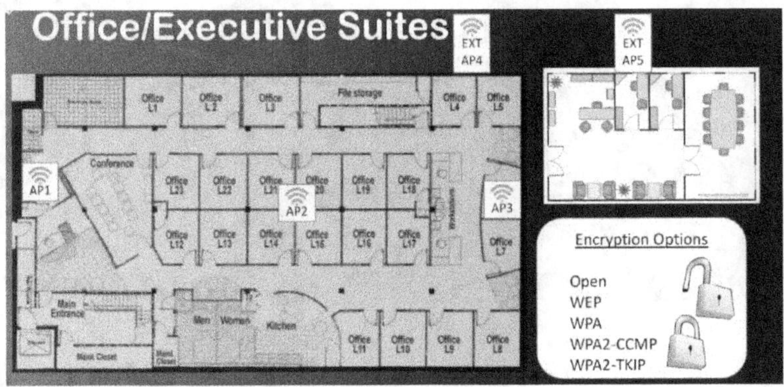

Which of the following is the BEST encryption from the options below to maximize network security between AP4 and AP5?

1. Open
2. WEP
3. WPA
4. WPA2-CCMP
5. WPA2-TKIP

Correct Answer(s): 4

Explanation:

WPA2-CCMP is the most secure option of the ones presented here. Open provides no encryption or confidentiality. WEP is considered weak and breakable. WPA is weak due to its TKIP implementation, and this weakeness carried over into WPA2-TKIP. Therefore, WPA2-CCMP is the most secure and provides the required level of confidentiality for this scenario.

QUESTION 2:

(This is a simulated Performance-Based Question.)

The company's corporate headquarters provided your branch office a portion of their Class C subnet to use at a new office location. You must allocate the minimum number of addresses using CIDR notation in order to accommodate each department's needs.

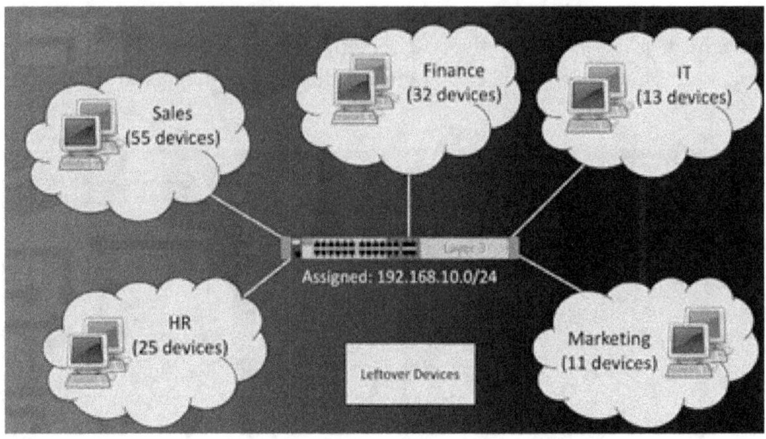

What is the correct CIDR notation for the Marketing department's subnet which requires 11 devices?

1. /25
2. /26
3. /27
4. /28
5. /29
6. /30

Correct Answer(s): 4

Explanation:

Since the Marketing department needs 11 devices plus a network ID and broadcast IP, it will require 13 IP addresses. The smallest subnet that can fit 13 IPs is a /28 (16 IPs).

QUESTION 3:

You are configuring a network to utilize SNMPv3 to send information from your network devices back to a SNMP manager. Which of the following SNMP options should you enable to ensure the data is transferred confidentially?

1. authPriv
2. authNoPriv
3. authProtect
4. authEncrypt

Correct Answer(s): 1

Explanation:

In SNMPv3, the authPriv option ensures that the communications are sent with authentication and privacy. This uses MD5 and SHA for authentication and DES and AES for privacy and encryption.

QUESTION 4:

You are working as a wireless networking technician and running a wireless controller to aid in the administration of the network. You supervisor has requested that you implement a centralized authentication service. Which of the following devices should you install and configure if you want to decrease the amount of time spent administering the network while still providing a centralized authentication service for your users?

1. Layer 3 switch
2. Proxy server
3. RADIUS server
4. VPN concentrator

Correct Answer(s): 3

Explanation:

A Remote Authentication Dial-In User Service (RADIUS) server will enable the wireless clients to communicate with a central server to authenticate users and authorize their access to the requested system or service. None of the other options presented are designed to support centralized authentication services by themselves, but instead use a protocol like RADIUS to perform those functions.

QUESTION 5:

A new network administrator is hired to replace a consultant that has been running the network for several months and whose contract was just cancelled. After a month of working on the network, the new network administrator realized there are some network issues and configuration changes in the server settings. The log files on the servers do not contain any error messages related to the issues or changes. What could be the problem?

1. TACACS+\RADIUS misconfiguration is causing logs to be erased
2. ICMP ping of death is resetting DHCP and DNS on the server
3. A backdoor has been installed to access the network
4. The last ACL on the router is set to Deny All

Correct Answer(s): 3

Explanation:

A hacker or the previous administrator (consultant) left a piece of software or an SSH protocol to be able to allow themselves access to the network in order to change the server settings. The consultant may be disgruntled that their contract was cancelled and that the new network administrator was hired to replace them.

QUESTION 6:

Lynne is a home user who would like to share music throughout the computers in her house using an external USB hard drive connected to a router that she purchased over a year ago. The manufacturer states that the router is capable of recognizing drives up to 4TB in size, but she cannot get her 3TB drive to show up on the network. What should Lynne do to fix this problem?

1. Load the latest hardware drivers for her USB drive
2. Install the latest OS on her computers
3. Download the latest playback software for her music files
4. Flash the latest firmware for her router

Correct Answer(s): 4

Explanation:

Routers can be updated by conducting a firmware flash. This is similar to upgrading or patching your computer's operating system, or even updating a device driver. By flashing the firmware, it can provide the ability to communicate with newer devices.

QUESTION 7:

Which device actively defends the network by detecting threats and shutting down ports or changing configurations to prevent attacks?

1. Honeypot
2. IPS
3. Firewall
4. IDS

Correct Answer(s): 2

Explanation:

Intrusion Protection Systems (IPS) can reconfigure themselves based on the threats experienced. Firewalls maintain a static configuration.

QUESTION 8:

Which of the following ports are used to provide secure remote connection sessions over the Internet?

1. 22
2. 25
3. 80
4. 23

Correct Answer(s): 1

Explanation:

Port 22 is used by Secure Shell (SSH) to securely create communication sessions over the Internet for remote access to a server or system. Telnet used to be used over port 23, but it is insecure and doesn't provide an encrypted tunnel like SSH does. Port 25 is for SMTP, and Port 80 is for HTTP, neither of which provide an encrypted tunnel, either.

QUESTION 9:

Barbara, an employee, has properly connected her personal wireless router to a network jack inside her office. The router is unable to get a DHCP address even though her corporate laptop can get a DHCP address when connected to the same jack. Barbara checked the router's configuration to ensure it is setup to obtain a DHCP address. Which of the following is the MOST likely reason that the router is not getting a DHCP address?

1. The administrator has enabled DHCP snooping on the network
2. The administrator is blocking DHCP requests that originate from access points
3. The administrator is blocking the wireless router's MAC address using MAC filtering
4. The Administrator has implemented a feature that only allows whitelist MAC addresses to connect to the network

Correct Answer(s): 4

Explanation:

Whitelisting specific MAC addresses is a security measure implemented by the administrator in order to grant access to a specific user only. It avoids a person with malicious intention to access the corporate network. Since the router has a different MAC address, it is being blocked from connecting to the wired network.

QUESTION 10:

A network technician needs to monitor the network to find a user that is browsing websites that are against the company policy. What should the technician use to view the website and find the user browsing it?

1. SNMP GET
2. Top listener tool
3. Intrusion detection system
4. Packet sniffer

Correct Answer(s): 4

Explanation:

Packet Sniffers can capture and analyze network user traffic. This information can be queried to view website addresses, contents, and sometimes even the password information. This differs from an intrusion detection system in that IDS' wait to receive implicitly-malicious data in a network prior to logging the event.

QUESTION 11:

You are trying to increase the security of your network by implementing a system of two-factor authentication (2FA). Which of the following authentication factors should you choose to meet this requirement?

1. Smartcard and PIN
2. Facial scan and fingerprint
3. Key fob and smartcard

4. Username and password

Correct Answer(s): 1

Explanation:

Two-factor authentication (also known as 2FA) is a method of confirming a user's claimed identity by using a combination of two different factors: (1) something you know, (2) something you have, or (3) something you are. Out of the options provided, only a smartcard (something you have) and a PIN (something you know) meet the requirements of 2FA. If you have two factors from the same type/category, like something you know (username and password), this is only considered a single factor of authentication.

QUESTION 12:

A new piece of malware is attempting to exfiltrate user data through hiding the traffic and sending it over a TLS-encrypted outbound traffic over random ports. What technology would be able to detect and block this type of traffic?

1. Intrusion detection system
2. Application aware firewall
3. Stateful packet inspection
4. Stateless packet inspection

Correct Answer(s): 2

Explanation:

A Web Application Firewall (WAF) or Application Aware Firewall would be able to detect both the accessing of random ports and TLS encryption, and could identify it as suspicious, whereas Stateless would inspect port number being used by the traffic leaving. IDS only analyzes incoming traffic, therefore would not be able to see this activity as suspicious.

QUESTION 13:

A network administrator needs to install a centrally-located firewall that needs to block specific incoming and outgoing IP addresses without denying legitimate return traffic. Which type of firewall should the administrator install?

1. A host-based firewall
2. A stateful network-based firewall
3. A host-based stateful firewall
4. A stateless network-based firewall

Correct Answer(s): 2

Explanation:

A stateful firewall enhances security through the use of packet filtering and these types of firewalls also keep track of outbound requests and open the port for the returning traffic to enter the network.

QUESTION 14:

A client has combined the voice-data circuit from a provider and is getting a maximum download and upload speeds of 2.0Mbps. Which type of service is MOST likely being used by the client?

1. ADSL
2. T1
3. E1
4. VDSL

Correct Answer(s): 3

Explanation:

E1 service provides symmetric 2.0 Mbps of data service. It can handle voice and digital services (with a mix-n-match service). E1 is the European signal of DS1. E1 has higher bandwidth than T1 because T1 reserves bits for overhead. VDSL and ADSL provide different upload and download rates, but this question shows that a symmetric upload and download rate was used.

QUESTION 15:

What allows a telecommunication company to remotely test circuits of customers?

1. VLAN configuration
2. Toner Probe
3. RDP
4. Smart Jack

Correct Answer(s): 4

Explanation:

Smart jacks have built-in remote diagnostics.

QUESTION 16:

You have been asked to add an entry to your DNS records to allow SMTP traffic to be sent out using your domain name. Which type of record should you add to your DNS record?

1. CNAME
2. A
3. MX
4. AAAA

Correct Answer(s): 3

Explanation:

A MX record is used for outgoing (SMTP) and incoming (POP3/IMAP) traffic. An A record associates your domain name with an IPv4 address. An AAAA record associates your domain name with an IPv6 address. A CNAME record is canonical name or alias name, which associates one domain name as an alias of another (like beta.diontraining.com and www.diontraining.com could both refer to the same website using a CNAME).

QUESTION 17:

Your company has just installed a new web server that will allow inbound connections over port 80 from the internet while not being able to accept any connections from the internal network. You have been asked where to place the web server in the network architecture and how to configure the ACL rule to support the requirements. The current network architecture is segmented using a firewall to create the following three zones: ZONE INTERFACE IP address PUBLIC eth0 66.13.24.16/30 DMZ eth1 172.16.1.1/24 PRIVATE eth2 192.168.1.1/24 Based on the requirements and current network architecture above, what is the BEST recommendation?

1. Put the server in the DMZ with an inbound rule from eth1 to eth0 that allows port 80 traffic to the server's IP
2. Put the server in the PUBLIC zone with an inbound rule from eth0 to eth1 that allows port 80 traffic to the server's IP
3. Put the server in the DMZ with an inbound rule from eth0 to eth1 that allows port 80 traffic to the server's IP
4. Put the server in the PRIVATE zone with an inbound rule from eth0 to eth1 that allows port 80 traffic to the server's IP

Correct Answer(s): 3

Explanation:

Since the new web server needs to not allow traffic from the internal network (PRIVATE), you should place it in the DMZ. Then, you should add an ACL entry to the firewall that allows traffic from eth0 (PUBLIC, the internet) to the server's IP within the DMZ (eth1). Most firewalls utilize an implicit deny policy, so all other ports from the eth0 will be blocked, as well as all ports from eth2.

QUESTION 18:

You have been asked to connect three 802.11a devices to an 802.11g access point that is configured with WEP. The devices are within 20 feet of the access point, but they are still unable to associate with the access point. Which of the following is the MOST likely cause of the devices being unable to associate with the WAP?

1. Interference
2. Frequency mismatch
3. Signal loss
4. Mismatched encryption

Correct Answer(s): 2

Explanation:

802.11a operates in the 5 GHz band while 802.11g operates in the 2.4 GHz band. Therefore, 802.11a devices will be unable to communicate with 802.11b or 802.11g access point.

QUESTION 19:

One of the routers in your network just failed. You have been asked to replace it with the same model router from the spare inventory closet as part of an emergency change request. You find the new router in the closet and notice it was signed into inventory 13 months ago. You install the router and attempt to enable HTTPS in the configuration to allow for remote access. The failed router had this capability, but this spare does not even though they are the exact same model and were purchased at the same time. What should you do to enable the HTTPS access for this router?

1. Perform a factory reset
2. Update the firmware
3. Enable HTTP instead
4. Reboot the router

Correct Answer(s): 2

Explanation:

Since the new router was pulled from your spare inventory closet, it is likely using an older and out of date version of the firmware. You should update the firmware for this router and then check if the HTTPS can be enabled again.

QUESTION 20:

A common technique used by malicious individuals to perform a man-in-the-middle attack on a wireless network is:

1. ARP cache poisoning
2. Amplified DNS attacks
3. Session hijacking
4. Creating an evil twin

Correct Answer(s): 4

Explanation:

Evil Twin access points are the most common way to perform a man-in-the-middle attack on a wireless network.

QUESTION 21:

A technician needs to add new features to existing hardware devices. Which of the following should be performed to add the new features?

1. Firmware updates
2. Changing to IPv6
3. Cloning
4. Vulnerability patching

Correct Answer(s): 1

Explanation:

To add new features to existing hardware devices, updating the firmware is always a must to mitigate any vulnerabilities.

QUESTION 22:

Rick is upset that he was passed over for a promotion. He decides to take revenge on his nemesis, Mary, who got the job instead of him. Rick sets up a man-in-the-middle attack against Mary's computer by redirecting any layer 2 traffic destined for the gateway to his own computer first. Rick is careful to only affect the traffic associated with Mary's computer and not the entire network. Which type of man-in-the-middle attack is Rick conducting against Mary?

1. IP spoofing
2. MAC spoofing
3. ARP cache poisoning
4. Evil twin

Correct Answer(s): 3

Explanation:

Based on the scenario, we can eliminate evil twin (which is focused on wireless access points) and IP spoofing (since this affects layer 3 traffic). While MAC spoofing the address of the gateway might work, it would also affect every computer on this subnet. By conducting an ARP cache poisoning attack, Rick can poison the cache and replace Mary's computer's MAC association with his own, allowing him to become the man-in-the-middle between Mary and the default gateway.

QUESTION 23:

A home user reports to a network technician that the Internet is slow. The network administrator discovers that multiple unknown devices are connected to the access point. What is MOST likely the cause?

1. An evil twin has been implemented
2. A successful WPS attack has occurred
3. The user is experiencing ARP poisoning
4. The user is connected to a botnet

Correct Answer(s): 2

Explanation:

Successful WPS attacks happen when the default username/password etc. has not been changed or reconfigured on the router. If your default username/password hasn't been changed, anybody can get into the settings and open the network. This is why additional unknown devices are on the network.

QUESTION 24:

A network administrator needs to allow employees to upload files to a remote server securely. What port should be allowed through the firewall?

1. 21
2. 22
3. 25
4. 161

Correct Answer(s): 2

Explanation:

Normally, port 21 is used for the FTP (File Transfer Protocol) to transfer files between computers and a remote server, but it does so over an unencrypted connection (and is therefore not secure). Therefore, it is a better idea to use port 22 which will allow a user to use SFTP (Secure FTP) or SCP (Secure Copy) to transfer a file from a computer to a remote server over an encrypted SSL/TLS tunnel.

QUESTION 25:

Which of the following is designed to keep system's uptime running in the event of a disaster?

1. High availability
2. Load balancing
3. Quality of service
4. Caching engines

Correct Answer(s): 1

Explanation:

If a network switch or router stops operating correctly (meaning that a network fault occurs), communication through the network could be disrupted, resulting in a network becoming unavailable to its users. Therefore, network availability, called uptime, is a major design consideration.

QUESTION 26:

(This is a simulated Performance-Based Question.) What is the correct color scheme for Pin 1 to Pin 8 for a T-568B connector?

1. blue, white/blue, orange, white/brown, brown , white/green, green, orange/white
2. white/green, green, orange/white, blue, white/blue, orange, white/brown, brown
3. white/orange, orange, white/green, blue, white/blue, green, white/brown, brown

4. white/green, green , white/orange, orange, blue, white/blue, white/brown, brown

Correct Answer(s): 3

Explanation:

You need to have the T-568-A and T-568-B standards memorized before test day, because you may be asked to perform a drag and drop exercise of placing the right colored wires into the right pin numbers based on a T-568A or T-568B connector. Remember, a straight through cable will have T-568B one both ends. If you are asked to make a cross-over cable, you need a T-568A on one side and a T-568B on the other side.

QUESTION 27:

(This is a simulated Performance-Based Question.) What ports do FTP and SFTP utilize?

1. 20, 21
2. 21, 22
3. 22, 23
4. 21, 23

Correct Answer(s): 2

Explanation:

FTP (File Transfer Protocol) uses port 20 and 21. SFTP (Secure File Transfer Protocol) uses port 22. If this was a question on the real exam, you would see a list of ports on one side and a list of protocols on the other, and you would drag and drop each one to match them up. (It might also have 4-6 different pairs to match up.)

QUESTION 28:

(This is a simulated Performance-Based Question.)

You are testing a cable you found in your network closet. You connect a cable tester to both sides of the cable to verify the pinout of the Ethernet cable. After testing each pin, your cable tester gives you the following output:

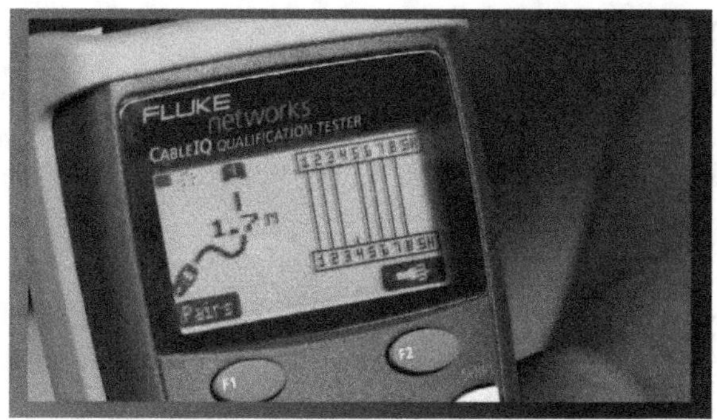

Based on this output, what kind of cable is it?

1. Patch cable
2. Crossover cable
3. Rollover cable
4. RG-6 cable

Correct Answer(s): 1

Explanation:

This is a patch cable (also known as a straight throught cable), as indicated by the matching of the Tx and Rx pins (pins 1, 2, 3, and 6) on both sides of the cable.

QUESTION 29:

Which type of network geography is used to connect various circuits between remote locations?

1. WAN
2. PAN
3. WLAN
4. LAN

Correct Answer(s):

Explanation:

WAN because to connect various circuits between remote locations, a Wide Area is required. Local can only be within a limited small area. A PAN is used for very small areas. A WLAN is a wireless LAN.

QUESTION 30:

A network administrator wants to implement a centralized monitoring solution that utilizes push alerts sent from the client to a server. Which of the following should be implemented within the network?

1. SNMP
2. SMTP
3. NIDS
4. SMS

Correct Answer(s): 1

Explanation:

The keyword is MONITORING. SNMP stands for Simple Network Management Protocol. SMTP is simple mail TRANSPORT protocol. NIDS is network intrusion detection system and SMS is short message service. So, knowing what all of them stand for helps you to understand if the goal is simply to manage the server and send alerts from client to server. Based on these information, SNMP is the best choice.

QUESTION 31:

Which of the following wireless technologies use MIMO on non-overlapping channels to increase the bandwidth of the wireless network?

1. 802.11a
2. 802.11b
3. 802.11g
4. 802.11n

Correct Answer(s): 4

Explanation:

802.11n introduced support for MIMO on non-overlapping channels as a method to increase the bandwidth available for the wireless network. This is also supported in 802.11ac (MU-MIMO), which was the next version released after 802.11n. The other wireless networking technologies (a/b/g) do not support MIMO.

QUESTION 32:

You have been asked by your supervisor, Martha, to ensure that you enable 802.3af on a managed switch. Which of the following features does Martha want you to enable?

1. PoE
2. Port bonding
3. VLAN
4. Trunking

Correct Answer(s): 1

Explanation:

Power over Ethernet (PoE) is defined by the IEEE 802.3af standard. PoE+ is defined by the IEEE 802.3at standard.

QUESTION 33:

What can be issued from the command line to find the layer 3 hops to a remote destination?

1. traceroute
2. nslookup
3. ping
4. netstat

Correct Answer(s): 1

Explanation:

Traceroute will determine every hop between the host and the destination using ICMP.

QUESTION 34:

A network technician is troubleshooting connectivity problems between switches but suspects the ports are not properly labeled. What option will help to quickly identify the switches connected to each port?

1. Configure TACACs+ on each network device
2. Enable a discovery protocol on the network devices.
3. Configure each uplink to send LACP discovery units.
4. Enable a packet sniffer on each network device's uplink port.

Correct Answer(s): 2

Explanation:

By enabling a discovery protocol on the network devices, the technician will be able to get detailed information such as the IP addresses, system version, and the type of device information from supporting devices directly connected to the discovery protocol, therefore providing information about the specific routers.

QUESTION 35:

Multiple students within a networking lab are required to simultaneously access a single switch remotely. The administrator checks and confirms that the switch can be accessed using the console, but currently only one student can log in at a time. What should be done to fix this issue?

1. Increase installed memory and install a larger flash module
2. Increase the number of VLANs configured on the switch
3. Decrease the number of VLANs configured on the switch
4. Increase the number of virtual terminals available

Correct Answer(s): 4

Explanation:

You can set a limit of how many virtual terminals can simultaneously connect to a switch. Here, the limit is set to one and we should increase it to solve the issue.

QUESTION 36:

Which of the following is an example of a valid IPv4 address?

1. 192:168:1:55
2. 192.168.1.254
3. 00:AB:FA:B1:07:34
4. ::1

Correct Answer(s): 2

Explanation:

An IPv4 address consists of 32 bits. IPv4 addresses are written in dotted octet notation, such as 192.168.1.254.

QUESTION 37:

A user has installed a new wireless printer on the network. The user cannot get it connected to the Internet, but can print locally. All other office users can reach the Internet, but cannot connect to the new wireless printer. All users are wireless in this part of the office. What MOST likely has occurred?

1. They installed the printer in infrastructure mode

2. They installed the printer in the wrong subnet
3. They misconfigured the gateway on the wireless printer
4. They installed the printer in ad-hoc mode

Correct Answer(s): 4

Explanation:

The printer is most likely in ad-hoc mode, which is also known as IBSS. In this type of network, devices talk directly to each other but have no connection outside of this "self-created" network.

QUESTION 38:

The Chief Information Officer (CIO) in your company has been trying to convince the Chief Security Officer (CSO) that the company should move its data to a SaaS solution in order to some money in the budget. The CSO is hesitant to move all of the company's data because she is concerned with the risk involved in moving the corporation's sensitive data to a SaaS solution. The CSO has been asked for a reason behind her fears. Which of the following might be her response?

1. The SaaS solution is incompatible with our current network
2. Migrating all of our data to a SaaS solution will result in a loss of full control over our data and resources
3. Migrating our data to a SaaS solution will result in decreased performance in our internal network
4. Migrating to a SaaS solution will put us at a higher risk of exposure to malware and hackers

Correct Answer(s): 2

Explanation:

Migrating all of the corporate data to a SaaS solution will result in a loss of full control over the data and its protection. If the company intends to move sensitive data to a cloud-based solution, it should seek out a private cloud solution or a PaaS/IaaS solution instead since it will allow them to retain much more control over their data. As for exposure to malware and hackers, there is no evidence that cloud solutions are more exposed than on-premise solutions. Since the proposal is to migrate information out of the internal network, this should not decrease performance but instead increase it. Also, since a SaaS is proposed, there is not an incompatibility issues since SaaS solutions are almost always web-based solutions, and therefore compatible with any web browser.

QUESTION 39:

Jason just got into his car and paired his smartphone to his car's stereo. Which of the following types of networks was just created?

1. LAN
2. PAN
3. WAN
4. MAN

Correct Answer(s): 2

Explanation:

PAN is short for Personal Area Network. Personal area networks generally cover a range of a few centimeters up to around 10 meters (33 feet). Bluetooth, Infrared, or USB connections are usually used to form a PAN.

QUESTION 40:

You have been asked by the server administrators to open the default port on the firewall for their new DNS server. Which of the following ports should you set as ALLOW in the ACL?

1. 53
2. 67
3. 110
4. 3389

Correct Answer(s): 1

Explanation:

Port 53 is used for DNS. Port 67 is used for DHCP. Port 110 is used for POP3. Port 3389 is used for RDP.

QUESTION 41:

A college needs to provide wireless connectivity in a cafeteria with a minimal number of WAPs. What type of antenna will provide the BEST coverage?

1. High gain
2. Bidirectional
3. Dipole
4. Omni-directional

Correct Answer(s): 1

Explanation:

High gain antennas put out increased signal strengths and therefore can reach further with less WAPs.

QUESTION 42:

Your router has been turning itself off and on again for a few weeks. You begin to think back to when these issues are occurring and remember that each time it occurs that the lights also become dimmer momentarily. You hook up a device to monitor the power being supplied to the router and identify that brownouts are frequently occurring, resulting in the power cycling of the router. What should you (a network technician) do to solve this problem?

1. Install an upgraded router
2. Install a surge protector
3. Install a UPS
4. Install a new electrical outlet

Correct Answer(s): 3

Explanation:

The best solution would be to install an UPS. Since you are a network technician and not an electrician, you should not attempt to install a new electrical circuit. The other two options would not solve this problem.

QUESTION 43:

An end user receives a new computer and now is unable to connect to a database using ODBC. Other users are able to connect successfully, and the network technician is able to successfully ping the database server but still is unable to connect. What might have caused this issue?

1. Missing IP routes on router
2. Wrong default gateway address
3. Software firewall is blocking ports
4. Failing network interface card

Correct Answer(s): 3

Explanation:

A change in the firewall settings to allow access to the specified ports will fix the problem. It appears the default firewall on this new computer is blocking the port used to communicate with the database server.

QUESTION 44:

A network's design includes gateways connecting an assembly-line network. The assembly-line network uses specialized cabling and interfaces to allow the assembly-line robots to communicate with one another. Which type of network would you classify this design as?

1. CSU/DSU
2. SCADA/ICS
3. IS-IS
4. LAN

Correct Answer(s): 2

Explanation:

SCADA/ICS is used in industrial control systems, such as an assembly-line network.

QUESTION 45:

You have just upgraded a small office LAN switch. When you finish, a user states they can no longer access the network. You check the user's workstation, but do not see any LED lights lit on their NIC. What should you check next?

1. Verify the switch is connected to the router
2. Verify the device is using the correct cable type
3. Verify the NIC is operating properly
4. Verify the network cable is attached to the new switch

Correct Answer(s): 4

Explanation:

Since the workstation was working yesterday but now it isn't because you upgraded the switch, you should first double check what changed. In this case, you unplugged the old switch and connected the new switch. It is likely that you didn't fully plug the cable back into the new switch after the upgrade. This would lead to no LED lights being lit on the workstation's NIC. Similarly, if you recently moved a workstation,

you would want to double check the cable connection on the workstation itself. This
is most likely a layer 1 issue.

QUESTION 46:

Several users at an adjacent office building report connectivity issues after a new
building was built in-between the two offices. The network technician has
determined the adjacent office building is connected to the main office building via
an 802.11ac bridge. The network technician logs into the AP and confirms the SSID,
encryption, and channels are all correct. Which of the following is MOST likely the
cause of this issue?

1. Device saturation
2. Antenna type
3. Bandwidth saturation
4. Interference

Correct Answer(s): 4

Explanation:

The most likely reason is interference from the new building being placed between
the signal path. By process of elimination: Device saturation involves too many
devices with too few sources, antenna type restricts the direction for the data to
travel and the bandwidth saturation occurs if too many devices are on one WAN
link.

QUESTION 47:

An employee of a highly-secure company needs to use facial recognition in addition
to username/password to successfully establish a VPN. What BEST describes this
methodology?

1. PKI
2. Federated identity
3. Two-factor authentication
4. Biometric authentication

Correct Answer(s): 3

Explanation:

This would classify best as two-factor authentication, since it requires "something
you are" (face) and "something you know" (username/password) for successful
authentication to occur.

QUESTION 48:

Your network has been the victim of data breach. Your company has hired an incident response team to help control the damage of the breach and restore the network to its full functionality. The incident response team wants to connect a packet capture device to the switch that connects your servers to the DMZ. Which of the following should be configured to ensure the packet capture device can receive all the network traffic going to and from the servers?

1. 802.1q
2. 802.1x
3. Port mirroring
4. Port security

Correct Answer(s): 3

Explanation:

Port Mirroring, also known as SPAN (Switched Port Analyzer), is a method of monitoring network traffic. With port mirroring enabled, the switch sends a copy of all network packets seen on one port (or an entire VLAN) to another port, where the packet can be analyzed. In this case, you can connect the packet capture device to the SPAN port (mirrored port) to collect all the network traffic for later analysis.

QUESTION 49:

OFDM, QAM and QPSK are all examples of what wireless technology?

1. Frequency
2. Modulation
3. RF interference
4. Spectrum

Correct Answer(s): 2

Explanation:

Common types of modulation include Orthogonal frequency-division multiplexing (OFDM), Quadrature Amplitude Modulation (QAM), and Quadrature Phase-shift keying (PSK).

QUESTION 50:

You are working as a wireless networking technician and have been sent to a user's home to install a brand new 802.11 AC WAP to replace their old WAP. To ensure all of the current devices on the network will automatically connect to the new network, you set the SSID, encryption type, and password to the exact same ones as the old WAP. You turn the new WAP on and notice most of the devices connect automatically, but one older wireless printer simply won't connect. You notice that the printer is about 7 years old, but the user says it has always worked great over the old wireless network. What is the MOST likely reason that the printer will not connect to the new WAP?

1. You forgot to set the channel properly
2. The power level on the WAP is too low
3. The password on the WAP was changed
4. There is a mismatch in frequencies

Correct Answer(s): 4

Explanation:

Wireless B/G networks utilize 2.4 Ghz, while Wireless AC uses 5.0 Ghz. Wireless N has the ability to support both 2.4 ghz and 5.0 Ghz frequencies. The most likely cause of the issue is that the older WAP supported 2.4 Ghz (for older devices) and 5.0 Ghz (for newer devices). Since you installed a brand new 802.11 AC WAP, it is only broadcasting at 5.0 Ghz, which prevents the older printer from connecting due to a frequency mismatch.

QUESTION 51:

You are configuring a point-to-point link and want to ensure it is configured for the most efficient use of your limited pool of available public IP addresses. Which of the following subnet masks would be BEST to use in this scenario?

1. /24
2. /28
3. /29
4. /30

Correct Answer(s): 4

Explanation:

The most efficient subnet mask for a point-to-point link is actually a /31 subnet, which only provides 2 addresses. This will only work if both routers are using a newer routing protocol like OSPF, IS-IS, EIGRP, or RIPv2 (or above). The tried and true method is to use a /30, though, which uses 4 IP addresses. The first is the network IP, the last is the broadcast, and the other 2 IPs can be assigned to the routers on either end of the point-to-point network. For the exam, if you see the option of /30 or /31, remember, they can be used for point-to-point networks.

QUESTION 52:

You are working at the service desk as a network security technician and just received the following email from an end user who believes a phishing campaign is being attempted. ********************** From: user@diontraining.com To: abuse@diontraining.com Subject: You won a free iPhone! Dear Susan, You have won a brand new iPhone! Just click the following link to provide your address so we can ship it out to you this afternoon: (http://www.freephone.io:8080/winner.php) ********************** What should you do to prevent any other employees from accessing the link in the email above, while still allowing them access to any other webpages at the domain freephone.io?

1. Add http://www.freephone.io:8080/winner.php to the browser's group policy block list
2. Add DENY TCP http://www.freephone.io ANY EQ 8080 to the firewall ACL
3. Add DENY IP ANY ANY EQ 8080 to the IPS filter
4. Add http://www.freephone.io:8080/winner.php to the load balancer

Correct Answer(s): 1

Explanation:

There are two ways to approach this question. First, you can consider which is the right answer (if you know it). By adding the full URL of the phishing link to the browser's group policy block list (or black hole list), the specific webpage will be blocked from being accessed by the employees while allowing the rest of the freephone.io domain to be access. Now, why not just block the entire domain? Well, maybe the rest of the domain isn't suspect but just this one page is. (For example, maybe someone is using a legitimate site like GitHub to host their phishing campaign, therefore you only want to block their portion of GitHub.) The second approach to answering this question would be to rule out the incorrect answers. If you used DENY TCP to the firewall ACL answer, you would block all access to the domain, blocking legitimate traffic as well as the possible malicious activity. If you used the DENY IP ANY ANY to filter traffic at the IPS, you would block any IP traffic to ANY website over port 8080. If you added the link to the load balancer, this would not block it either. Therefore, we are only left with the correct answer of using a group policy in this case.

QUESTION 53:

Which of the following network geographies refer to a network that spans several buildings that are within walking distance of each other, such as at a business park?

1. CAN

2. WAN
3. PAN
4. MAN

Correct Answer(s): 1

Explanation:

A campus area network (CAN) is a network of multiple interconnected local area networks (LAN) in a limited geographical area. These are common in business parks and at colleges/universities.

QUESTION 54:

A network administrator updated an Internet server to evaluate some new features in the current release. A week after the update, the Internet server vendor warns that the latest release may have introduced a new vulnerability and a patch is not available for it yet. Which of the following should the administrator do to mitigate this risk?

1. Enable the host-based firewall on the Internet server
2. Enable HIPS to protect the server until the patch is released
3. Utilize WAF to restrict malicious activity to the Internet server
4. Downgrade the server and defer the new feature testing

Correct Answer(s): 4

Explanation:

Since the vendor stated that the new version introduces vulnerabilities in the environment, it is better to downgrade the server to the older and more secure version until a patch is available.

QUESTION 55:

A client reports that half of the office is unable to access a shared printer on the network. Which of the following should the network technician use to troubleshoot the issue?

1. Data backups
2. Network Diagrams
3. Baseline information
4. Vendor documentation

Correct Answer(s): 2

Explanation:

Network diagram is a visual representation of a computer network. Understanding all the connections is a fundamental step in network troubleshooting. This baseline information can be used for anticipating future problems, as well as planning for future growth.

QUESTION 56:

A technician is tasked with troubleshooting a network's slowness. While troubleshooting, the technician is unable to ping any external websites. Users report they are able to access the sites using the web browsers. What is the MOST likely cause?

1. ICMP traffic being blocked by the firewall
2. VLAN hopping
3. TACACS misconfiguration
4. MTU black hole

Correct Answer(s): 1

Explanation:

Many companies block ICMP at the firewall, causing PING to fail since it relies on ICMP. If the user can access the site in the web browser but not by PING, this is usually the cause.

QUESTION 57:

You have installed and configured a new wireless router. The clients and hosts can ping each other. The WAN connection is 10Gbp/s. The wired clients have fast connections, but the wireless clients are slow to ping and browse the Internet. Which of the following is MOST likely the cause of the slow speeds experienced by the wireless clients?

1. An access point experiencing RFI from fluorescent light bulbs
2. A router is on the incorrect LAN
3. A cable connection does not support wireless
4. A high signal-to-noise ratio on the wireless network

Correct Answer(s): 1

Explanation:

If interference in the wireless spectrum is occurring, more retransmissions will be needed (and thereby slowing speeds experienced). All the other answers will not cause a slow down of only the wireless network. And a high signal to noise ratio is a good thing on wireless networks.

QUESTION 58:

Which of the following WAN technologies would MOST likely be used to connect several remote branches that have no fiber or satellite connections?

1. OC12
2. POTS
3. WiMax
4. OC3

Correct Answer(s): 2

Explanation:

POTS is the Plain Old Telephone System, and is connected to almost every facility in the United States. DSL and dial-up services can be received over POTS.

QUESTION 59:

A network technician was tasked to install a network printer and share it to a group of five human resource employees. The technician plugged the device into a LAN jack, but was unable to obtain an IP address automatically. What is the cause of the problem?

1. Incorrect DNS records
2. Incorrect TCP port in ACL
3. Split horizon is disabled
4. DHCP scope is exhausted

Correct Answer(s): 4

Explanation:

The DHCP scope is used as a pool of IP addresses that can be assigned automatically. The issue might be that there are no more IP addresses left in the scope and it is therefore exhausted.

QUESTION 60:

You network is currently under attack from multiple hosts outside of the network. Which type of attack is most likely occurring?

1. DoS
2. Spoofing
3. DDoS
4. Wardriving

Correct Answer(s): 3

Explanation:

A Distributed Denial of Service (DDoS) attack occurs when multiple systems flood the bandwidth or resources of a targeted system or network. DoS and Spoofing attacks originate from a single host, while wardriving is focused on the surveillance and reconnaissance of wireless networks.

QUESTION 61:

Which of the following network devices would be considered a perimeter device and should be installed at the outermost part of the network?

1. Switch
2. Firewall
3. Bridge
4. Wireless Access Point

Correct Answer(s): 2

Explanation:

A firewall is considered a perimeter security device. It should be installed at the perimeter or boundary of a network to provide the maximum security to the network. Switches, bridges, and wireless access points are all considered internal network devices, and should not be installed at the outermost perimeter of the network.

QUESTION 62:

Which communication technology would MOST likely be used to increase bandwidth over an existing fiber optic network by combining multiple signals at different wavelengths?

1. DWDM

2. SONET
3. ADSL
4. LACP

Correct Answer(s): 1

Explanation:

Dense wavelength-division multiplexing (DWDM) is a high-speed optical network type commonly used in MANs (metropolitan area networks). DWDM uses as many as 32 light wavelengths on a single fiber, where each wavelength can support as many as 160 simultaneous connections.

QUESTION 63:

While implementing wireless access points into the network, one building is having connectivity issues due to light fixtures being replaced in the ceiling, while all other buildings' connectivity is performing as expected. Which of the following should be changed on the access point for the building with connection issues?

1. UTP patch cables
2. Antenna
3. Power adapter
4. Security standard

Correct Answer(s): 2

Explanation:

Since only one building is having the issue, it is likely an issue with the antenna having radio frequency interference.

QUESTION 64:

A company needs to implement stronger authentication by adding an authentication factor to their wireless system. The wireless system only supports WPA with pre-shared keys, but the back-end authentication system supports EAP and TTLS. What should the network administrator implement?

1. PKI with user authentication
2. 802.1x using EAP with MSCHAPv2
3. WPA2 with a complex shared key
4. MAC address filtering with IP filtering

Correct Answer(s): 2

Explanation:

Since the back end uses a RADIUS server for back-end authentication, the network administrator can install 802.1x using EAP with MSCHAPv2 for authentication.

QUESTION 65:

A network technician determines that two dynamically-assigned workstations have duplicate IP addresses. What command should the technician use to correct this issue?

        1.   ipconfig /all
        2.   ipconfig /dhcp
        3.   ipconfig /release; ipconfig /renew
        4.   ipconfig /renew

Correct Answer(s): 3

Explanation:

The first thing to do is to release that IP address using the command ipconfig /release. Next, the technician should dynamically assign another IP address using the command ipconfig /renew.

QUESTION 66:

A network administrator is troubleshooting an issue with unstable wireless connections in a residence hall. Users on the first and second floors report that the hall's SSID is not visible in the evenings. The network administrator has verified that the wireless system is operating normally. What is the cause of the issue being reported by the users?

        1.   Internet router maintenance is scheduled
        2.   An ARP attack is underway
        3.   The SSID is set to hidden
        4.   A jammer is being used

Correct Answer(s): 1

Explanation:

Process of elimination: the ARP attack would allow attackers to intercept data or stop all traffic; the SSID being set to hidden wouldn't just change during the day, and a jammer being used would show some possible "wrong" traffic in the logs of the wireless. Internet router maintenance would simply take the network down for the duration of the update/maintenance.

QUESTION 67:

You are creating a wireless link between two buildings in an office park utilizing the 802.11ac standard. The antenna chosen must have a small physical footprint and a minimal weight as it will be mounted on the outside of the building. Which type of antenna should you install?

1. Whip
2. Omni-directional
3. Parabolic
4. Patch

Correct Answer(s): 4

Explanation:

A patch antenna is a type of radio antenna with a low profile, which can be mounted on a flat surface. A patch antenna is typically mounted to a wall or a mast and provides coverage in a limited angle pattern. A yagi or directional antenna could also be used, but if the distance is smaller than about 300 feet between the buildings, using a patch antenna would be sufficient. For longer distances, a yagi would be utilized instead, but these do weight more and have a larger footprint.

QUESTION 68:

Your company has several small branch offices around the country, but you work as a network administrator at the centralized headquarters building. You need the capability of being able to remotely access any of the remote site's routers to configure the without having to fly to each location in person. Your company's CIO is worried that allowing remote access could allow an attacker to gain administrative access to the company's network devices. Which of the following is the MOST secure way to prevent this from occurring, while still allowing you to access the devices remotely?

1. Create an out-of-band management network
2. Install an out-of-band modem
3. Configure the remote router's ACLs to only permit Telnet traffic
4. Configure the remote router's ACLs to only permit HTTP traffic

Correct Answer(s): 1

Explanation:

You should create an out-of-band management network using a SSH (console) connection to the router. Telnet and HTTP are not encrypted channels and should not be used for remote connections. Using a modem is also a bad security practice, since these are subject to war dialing and provide very slow connectivity speeds.

QUESTION 69:

A facility would like to verify each individual's identity prior to allowing access to its server room and datacenter. Additionally, the building should ensure that users do not tailgate behind other users. What solution would BEST meet these requirements?

1. Implement a biometric reader at the datacenter entrance and require passage through a mantrap
2. Implement a security guard at the facility entrance and a keypad at the data center entrance
3. Implement a CCTV camera and a proximity reader at the data center entrance
4. Implement a biometric reader at the facility entrance and a proximity card at the data center entrance

Correct Answer(s): 1

Explanation:

A biometric reader would read the employee's fingerprints. A mantrap is most often used in physical security to separate non-secure areas from secure areas and prevent unauthorized access.

QUESTION 70:

Which of the following is MOST likely to use an RJ-11 connector to connect a computer to an ISP using a POTS line?

1. Multilayer switch
2. Access point
3. Analog modem
4. DOCSIS modem

Correct Answer(s): 3

Explanation:

An analog modem is a device that converts the computer's digital pulses to tones that can be carried over analog telephone lines, and vice versa. The other type of Internet connection that occurs over an RJ-11 (phone line) is DSL.

QUESTION 71:

A company is installing several APs for a new wireless system that requires users to authenticate to the domain. The network technician would like to authenticate to a central point. What solution would be BEST to achieve this?

1. TACACS+ device and RADIUS server
2. TACACS and proxy server
3. RADIUS server and access point
4. RADIUS server and network controller

Correct Answer(s): 3

Explanation:

A Remote Authentication Dial-in User Service (RADIUS) server provides AAA management for users connecting to a wired or wireless network, which includes the ability to authenticate users. As servers are inherently not built with wireless access capabilities, an access point would have to be included in the setup for the RADIUS to work correctly with wireless clients.

QUESTION 72:

A technician installs three new switches to a company's infrastructure. The network technician notices that all the switch port lights at the front of each switch flash rapidly when powered on and connected. Additionally, there are rapidly flashing amber lights on the switches when they started up the next day. What is happening to the switches?

1. The switches are running through their spanning tree process
2. The switches are having problems communicating with each other
3. The switches are connected and detected a spanning tree loop
4. The switches are not functioning properly and need to be disconnected

Correct Answer(s): 1

Explanation:

The switches use the spanning tree process to ensure no routing loops will occur.

QUESTION 73:

Your network security manager wants a monthly report of the security posture of all the assets on the network (e.g. workstations, servers, routers, switches, firewalls). The report should include any feature of a system or appliance that is missing a security patch, OS update, or other essential security feature, as well as its risk severity. Which solution would work best to find this data?

1. Security policy
2. Penetration test
3. Virus scan
4. Vulnerability scanner

Correct Answer(s): 4

Explanation:

A vulnerability scanner is a computer program designed to assess computers, computer systems, networks, or applications for weaknesses. Most vulnerability scanners also create an itemized report of their findings after the scan.

QUESTION 74:

The Chief Information Officer (CIO) wants to improve the security of the company's data. Which management control should be implemented to ensure employees are using encryption to transmit any sensitive information over the network?

1. Policies
2. VPN
3. HTTPS
4. Standards

Correct Answer(s): 1

Explanation:

Policies are plans that describe the goal of an established procedure (Acceptable use, Physical Security or VPN access), while the standards are the mechanisms implemented to achieve that goal. VPN and HTTPS are examples of standards.

QUESTION 75:

After a company rolls out software updates, Ann, a lab researcher, is no longer able to use the lab equipment connected to her PC. The technician contacts the vendor and determines there is an incompatibility with the latest version of the drivers. Which of the following should the technician perform in order to get the researcher back to work as quickly as possible?

1. Roll back the drivers to the previous version
2. Reset Ann's equipment configuration from a backup
3. Downgrade the PC to a working patch level
4. Restore Ann's PC to the last known good configuration

Correct Answer(s): 1

Explanation:

By rolling back the drivers, Ann would be able to use her lab equipment again. To roll back a driver in Windows means to return the driver to the version that was last installed for the device.

Practice Exam #3

QUESTION 1:

(This is a simulated Performance-Based Question. On the real certification exam, you will be asked to drag-and-drop the correct antennas onto the APs.)

Your company has purchased a new building down the street for its executive suites. You have been asked to select an antenna for AP1, AP2, and AP3 in order to establish a wireless connection inside the main building for visitors to use.

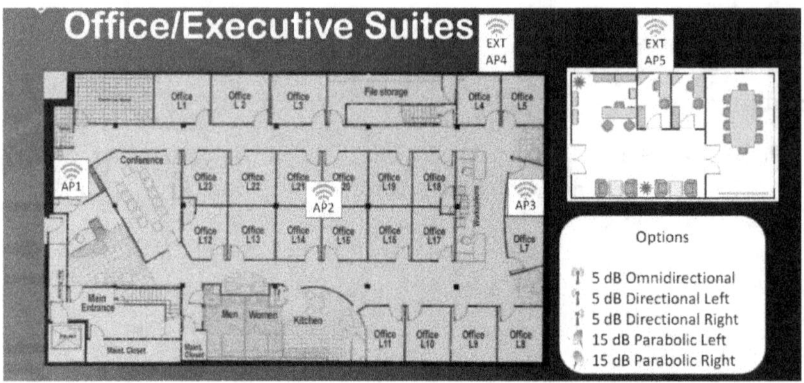

Which of the following is the BEST antenna configuration that will control the signal propagation and to keep the wireless signal from broadcasting outside of the main building?

1. 5 db Omnidirectional for AP1, 5 dB Directional Left for AP2, and 5 dB Directional Right for AP3
2. 5 db Directional Left for AP1, 5 dB Omnidirectional for AP2, and 5 dB Directional Right for AP3
3. 5 db Directional Right for AP1, 5 dB Omnidirectional for AP2, and 5 dB Directional Left for AP3
4. 5 db Directional Right for AP1, 5 dB Directional Left for AP2, and 5 dB Omnidirectional for AP3

Correct Answer(s): 3

Explanation:

For the best security and to keep the signal within the walls of the building, you should only use an omnidirectional antenna with AP2 and use directional antennas for AP1 and AP3. Using a Directional Right antenna on a left wall (AP1) and a Directional Left antenna on a right wall (AP3) assists with keeping the wireless signals inside the building and prevents security issues associated with your wireless signals being accessible from outside the building.

QUESTION 2:

(This is a simulated Performance-Based Question.)

The company's corporate headquarters provided your branch office a portion of their Class C subnet to use at a new office location. You must allocate the minimum number of addresses using CIDR notation in order to accommodate each department's needs.

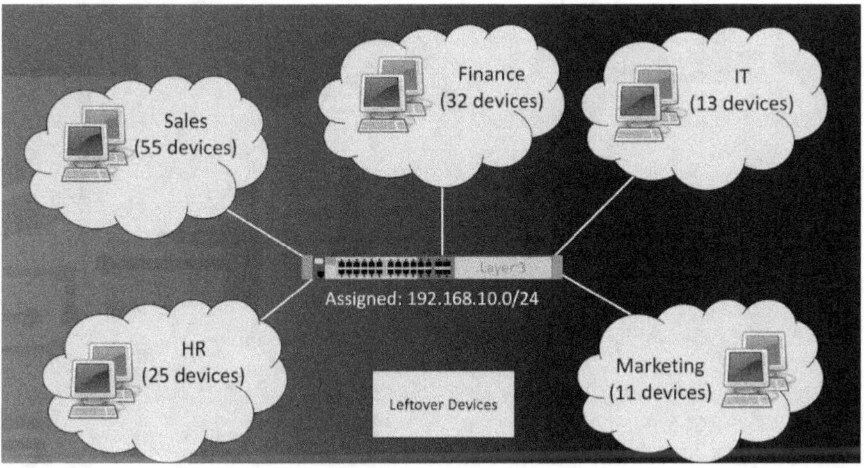

What is the correct CIDR notation for the Finance department's subnet which requires 32 devices?

1. /25
2. /26
3. /27
4. /28
5. /29
6. /30

Correct Answer(s): 2

Explanation:

Since the Finance department needs 32 devices plus a network ID and broadcast IP, it will require 34 IP addresses. The smallest subnet that can fit 34 IPs is a /26 (64 IPs).

QUESTION 3:

(This is a simulated Performance-Based Question.)

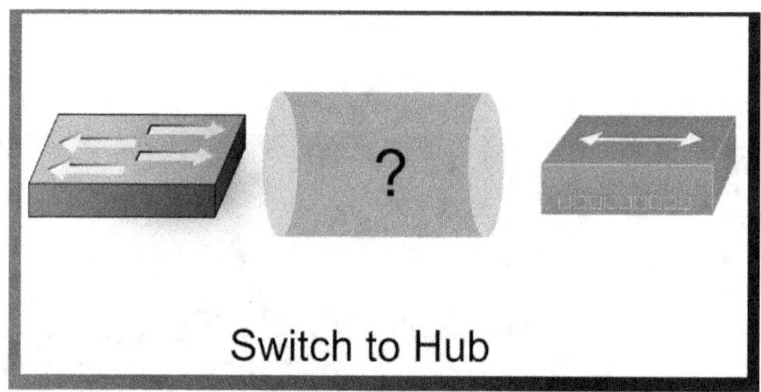

What type of cable would you use to connect a switch to a hub?

1. Crossover
2. RG-6
3. Rollover
4. RS-232

Straight-through

Correct Answer(s): 1

Explanation:

When connecting a switch to a hub, you can use a crossover cable (unless they support MDIX). If this was a real question on the exam, you would have the words provided in a list, and you would drag them below the appropriate drawing.

QUESTION 4:

(This is a simulated Performance-Based Question.)

You have been tasked with testing a CAT 5e network cable. After conducting the test using the tool provided by your manager, you see the following test results:

Cable Test Results		
1, 2	Open	3 ft
3, 6	Short	3 ft
4, 5	Open	3 ft
7, 8	Open	3 ft

What tool did you use to test the cable and get these results?

1. Crimper
2. Cable Certifier
3. Multimeter
4. Punch Down Tool
5. Protocol Analyzer
6. OTDR

Correct Answer(s): 2

Explanation:

Cable certifiers can provide a "pass" or "fail" status in accordance with the industry standards and can also show detailed information such as "open", "short", or the length of the cable. None of the other tools listed can provide you with this level of information.

QUESTION 5:

(This is a simulated Performance-Based Question.)

The results of the cable certifier are shown below:

Cable Test Results		
1, 2	Open	3 ft
3, 6	Short	3 ft
4, 5	Open	3 ft
7, 8	Open	3 ft

Using the results provided, was the cable properly crimped or not?

1. Cable was properly crimped
2. Cable was not properly crimped

Correct Answer(s): 2

Explanation:

Cable certifiers can provide a "pass" or "fail" status in accordance with the industry standards and can also show detailed information such as "open", "short", or the length of the cable. When a short is detected, but the full length of the cable is shown (3 ft), this indicates the cable was incorrectly crimped. In this case, it appears that pin 3 and pin 6 are both crimped into the same position in the RJ-45 connector, causing the short.

QUESTION 6:

Which of the following port or ports does SIP use?

1. 443
2. 389/636
3. 135/139/445
4. 5060/5061

Correct Answer(s): 4

Explanation:

SIP works with other protocols over 5060/5061. 443 is HTTPS, 389/636 is LDAP, and 135/139/445 is NetBIOS and SMB.

QUESTION 7:

What describes an IPv6 address of ::1?

1. Broadcast
2. Loopback
3. Classless
4. Multicast

Correct Answer(s): 2

Explanation:

In IPv6, ::1 is the loopback address, whereas in IPv4 it is 127.0.0.1. The loopback address is used to send a test signal sent to a network destination in order to diagnose problems.

QUESTION 8:

Dion Training has just installed a brand new email server. Which of the following DNS records would need to be created to allow the new server to receive email on behalf of diontraining.com?

1. CNAME
2. MX
3. PTR
4. A

Correct Answer(s): 2

Explanation:

An MX record is required in the DNS for a domain in order for the email server to accept emails on behalf of a registered domain name..

QUESTION 9:

If you have an ISDN or T-1 connection, it can deliver multiple voice calls over a copper wire using which of the following technologies?

1. CSMA/CD
2. Time division spread spectrum
3. Analog circuit switching
4. Time division multiplexing

Correct Answer(s): 4

Explanation:

Time-division multiplexing allows for two or more signals or bit streams to be transferred in what appears to be simultaneous sub-channels in one communication channel, but are physically taking turns on the channel. This is the technology used in a single PRI (ISDN or T-1) service to essentially share a single cable but pass multiple voice calls over it.

QUESTION 10:

Which of the following protocols are designed to avoid loops on a Layer 2 network?

1. OSPF
2. RIPv2
3. 802.1q
4. 802.1d

Correct Answer(s): 4

Explanation:

The Spanning Tree Protocol is part of the 802.1d standard and avoids loops in the switching network (layer 2).

QUESTION 11:

Which of the following describes the ID of a specified native VLAN when traffic passes over a trunk?

1. It becomes the gateway of last resort for the switch or router
2. It becomes the default VLAN for untagged frames
3. It becomes the priority ID for all the VLAN traffic across the device
4. It becomes the default gateway for the port or ports

Correct Answer(s): 2

Explanation:

Trunk ports carry all traffic, regardless of VLAN number, between all switches in a LAN. The VLAN designation for a trunk port is its native VLAN. If the trunk port has a native VLAN that differs from the tag placed on the frame as it entered the access port, the switch leaves the tag on the frame and sends the tagged frame along to the next switch or switches. If the trunk port's native VLAN is the same as the access ports VLAN, then the switch drops the tag and sends the untagged frame out the trunk port.

QUESTION 12:

A small law office has a network with three switches (8 ports), one hub (4 ports), and one router (2 ports). Switch 1 (switchport 8) is connected to an interface port (FastEthernet0/0) on the router. Switch 2 (switchport 8) and switch 3 (switchport 8) are connected to Switch 1 (switchports 1 and 2). The hub has three computers plugged into it on ports 1, 2, and 3. The fourth port on the hub is connected to the router's other interface port (FastEthernet0/1). Based on the configuration described here, how many broadcast domains are there within this network?

1. 1
2. 2
3. 5
4. 16
5. 28

Correct Answer(s): 2

Explanation:

A broadcast domain is a logical division of a computer network in which all nodes can reach each other by broadcast at the data link layer. A broadcast domain can be within the same LAN segment or it can be bridged to other LAN segments. Routers break up broadcast domains, therefore there are two broadcast domains in this network - one for each side of the router (the three switches makeup one broadcast domain, and the hub makes up the second broadcast domain).

QUESTION 13:

Which of the following wireless standards should you implement if the existing wireless network only allows for three non-overlapping channels and you need additional non-overlapping channels to prevent interference with neighboring businesses in your office building?

1. 802.11b
2. 802.11g
3. 802.11ac
4. 802.1q

Correct Answer(s): 3

Explanation:

Wireless B and G only support 3 non-overlapping channels (1, 6, 11). Wireless N and Wireless AC supports 5 GHz spectrum which provides dozens of non-overlapping channels. 802.1q is used for VLANs, and is not a wireless networking standard.

QUESTION 14:

Elizabeth was replacing a client's security device that protects their DMZ. The client has an application that allows external users to access the application remotely. After replacing the devices, the external users cannot connect remotely to the application anymore. Which of the following devices was MOST likely misconfigured and is now causing a problem?

1. Content filler
2. Firewall
3. DNS
4. DHCP

Correct Answer(s): 2

Explanation:

A firewall is an integral part of a DMZ. If configured correctly, it can regulate exactly what traffic and users are allowed to access the server. This is different from a content filter because a content filter simply denies traffic to a user based on content, but not access to a server. If the firewall ruleset was not configured to allow external users to access the application remotely, the default condition is to "deny by default".

QUESTION 15:

A technician is testing a new web-based tool capable of generating automatic teller machine (ATM) cash and service availability reports. The web-based tool was developed by a consortium of financial institutions. Which of the following cloud delivery models is being described in this scenario?

1. SaaS
2. Public
3. Community
4. PaaS

Correct Answer(s): 3

Explanation:

A community or private delivery model would work best. A community cloud in computing is a collaborative effort in which infrastructure is shared between several organizations from a specific community with common concerns (security, compliance, jurisdiction, etc.), whether managed internally or by a third-party and hosted internally or externally. The scenario described is a community cloud created tool by the banking industry.

QUESTION 16:

A technician needs to ensure wireless coverage in the green space near the center of the college campus. The antenna is being installed in the middle of the field on a pole. Which type of antenna should be installed to ensure maximum coverage?

1. Omnidirectional
2. Yagi
3. Unidirectional
4. Directional

Correct Answer(s): 1

Explanation:

Omnidirectional antennas send the signal out equally in all directions, therefore it will provide the best coverage since it is located in the center of the field.

QUESTION 17:

A technician suspects that the email system is slow due to an excessive amount of Spam being received. Which of the following should the technician do FIRST according to the troubleshooting methodology?

1. Verify full system functionality
2. Block incoming email
3. Establish a plan of action
4. Gather information

Correct Answer(s): 4

Explanation:

After identifying the problem (the server is slow), the next step is to gather information. This can be from various sources such as (but not limited to) users, logs and IP addresses. After information has been gathered, the technician should establish a plan of action to resolve the issue.

QUESTION 18:

You have just installed a new switch in your company's network closet. The switch connects to your router using a SFP port on both the router and switch. Unfortunately, you only had a long cable available to make the connection, so after running the cable from the rack containing the switch to the other rack containing the router you decide to coil up the excessive cable and use a zip tie to hold the coil to the side of the rack. You head back to your office, log into the switch over SSH, and check the log file. You notice that there are several messages indicating that the signal strength on the transmit portion of the SFP is registering as too weak. What is the BEST Correct Answer(s):

Explanation: for the cause of this error?

1. The SFP module has gone bad
2. You used a MMF cable instead of a SMF cable
3. The bend radius of the cable has been exceeded
4. You used a MTRJ cable instead of a ST cable

Correct Answer(s): 3

Explanation:

The most likely Correct Answer(s):

Explanation: is that you coiled up the excess cable too tightly and exceeded the bend radius for the cable. By doing this, you may have broken or cracked the fiber connected to the transmit portion of the SFP. It is unlikely that the SFP failed, since only the transmit portion is registering as weak. If you used the wrong type of cable (MTRJ vs ST), you would not have been able to connect it to the SFP module as it wouldn't fit. Similarly, if you used a MMF instead of a SMF cable, you would get no connection, not a weak connection.

QUESTION 19:

A company suffers an outage due to a bad module in a core switch. What is the NEXT step to conduct in troubleshooting?

1. Gather information, start at the top of the OSI model, and work down.
2. Establish a plan of action to solve the problem.
3. Establish a theory, identify the problem, duplicate the problem, test the theory, and repeat.
4. Gather information, start at the bottom of the OSI model, and work up.

Correct Answer(s): 2

Explanation:

The troubleshooting steps are to (1) Identify the problem, (2) Establish a theory of probable cause, (3) Test the theory to determine the cause, (4) Establish a plan of action to resolve the problem and identify potential effects, (5) Implement the solution or escalate as necessary, and (6) Verify full system functionality and if applicable implement preventative measures. Since the cause of the problem is already known (a bad module), we can skip directly to establishing a plan of action to solve the problem.

QUESTION 20:

Which of the following needs to be configured to allow jumbo frames on a network?

1. MTU
2. MAC
3. MIBS
4. IPS

Correct Answer(s): 1

Explanation:

MTU is the largest unit that can be transmitted across a network. If the MTU is set at a value above 1500, the network is configured to support jumbo frames.

QUESTION 21:

What is a connectionless protocol?

1. ICMP
2. SSL
3. TCP
4. SSH

Correct Answer(s): 1

Explanation:

A connectionless protocol is a form of data transmission in which data is transmitted automatically without determining whether the receiver is ready, or even whether a receiver exists. ICMP, UDP, IP, and IPX are well-known examples.

QUESTION 22:

Sarah connects a pair of switches using redundant links. When she checks the status of the links, one of them is not active, even when she changes ports. What MOST likely disabled the redundant connection to the other switch?

1. Spanning tree
2. IGRP routing
3. SSID mismatch
4. Port Mirroring

Correct Answer(s): 1

Explanation:

The purpose of spanning tree is to verify no loops exist in the network. If something isn't working, it's possibly because the switch detects that there's a loop in the redundant connections.

QUESTION 23:

A technician has finished configuring AAA on a new network device. However, the technician is unable to log into the device with LDAP credentials but is able to do so with a local user account. What is the MOST likely reason for the problem?

1. Username is misspelled in the device configuration file
2. IDS is blocking RADIUS
3. Shared secret key is mismatched
4. Group policy has not propagated to the device

Correct Answer(s): 3

Explanation:

AAA through RADIUS uses a Server Secret Key (a shared secret key). A secret key mismatch could cause login problems.

QUESTION 24:

An increased amount of web traffic to an e-commerce server is observed by a network administrator, but without an increase in the number of financial transactions. Which kind of attack might the company be experiencing?

1. Bluejacking
2. ARP cache poisoning
3. Phishing
4. DoS

Correct Answer(s): 4

Explanation:

A DoS attack or Denial-of-Service attack works by overloading a server with multiple requests (more than it can handle), thus eventually knocking the server offline.

QUESTION 25:

Your company's security policy states that its workstations must hide their internal IP addresses whenever they make a network request across the WAN. You have been asked to recommend a technology that would BEST implement this policy. Which of the following is the BEST solution for you to recommend?

1. NAT
2. DMZ
3. WPA
4. OSPF

Correct Answer(s): 1

Explanation:

Network address translation (NAT) is a method of remapping one IP address space into another by modifying network address information in the IP header of packets while they are in transit across a traffic routing device. By using NAT, you can have the internal IP address of each workstation mapped to a public IP address or port when it crosses the router to access the WAN.

QUESTION 26:

According to the OSI model, at which of the following layers is data encapsulated into a frame?

1. Layer 1
2. Layer 2
3. Layer 3
4. Layer 4

Correct Answer(s): 2

Explanation:

The data layer, or layer 2, is the second layer of the seven-layer OSI model. The data link layer encapsulates data into frames for delivery between nodes on the same network.

QUESTION 27:

A single mode fiber is no longer providing network connectivity to a remote site. What could be used to identify the location of the break?

1. MT-RJ

2. OTDR
3. Media Converter
4. Cable certifier

Correct Answer(s): 2

Explanation:

An optical time-domain reflectometer (OTDR) is an optoelectronic instrument used to characterize an optical fiber.

QUESTION 28:

What access control model will a network switch utilize if it requires multilayer switches to use authentication via RADIUS/TACACS+?

1. 802.1q
2. 802.3af
3. PKI
4. 802.1x

Correct Answer(s): 4

Explanation:

802.1x is the standard that is used for network authentication with RADIUS and TACACS+.

QUESTION 29:

You have just moved into a new apartment and need to get internet service installed. Your landlord has stated that you are not allowed to drill any holes to install new cables into the apartment. Luckily, your apartment already has cable TV installed. Which of the following technologies should you utilize to get your internet installed in your apartment?

1. Wireless router
2. DSL modem
3. Satellite modem
4. DOCSIS modem

Correct Answer(s): 4

Explanation:

DOCSIS (Data Over Cable Service Interface Specification) is an international telecommunications standard that permits the addition of high-bandwidth data transfer to an existing cable television system. It is employed by many cable television operators to provide Internet access over their existing hybrid fiber-coaxial (HFC) infrastructure. Most people today call these 'cable modems', but technically they are DOCSIS modems.

QUESTION 30:

You are currently troubleshooting a workstation in the office and determined that it is an issue with the cabling somewhere between the workstation and the switch. You have tested the patch cable from the workstation to the wall jack and it is not faulty. You want to check the port on the switch next, which of the following would BEST help you identify which switchport is associated with the workstation's wall jack?

1. Network baseline
2. Proper labeling
3. Inventory management
4. Standard procedures

Correct Answer(s): 2

Explanation:

You should always use proper labeling of your cables, wall jacks, and patch panels to make it easy to locate which switchport is associated with each portion of the cable distribution plant.

QUESTION 31:

Michael has been tasked with assigning two IP addresses to WAN interfaces on connected routers. In order to conserve address space, which of the following subnet masks should he use for this subnet?

1. /24
2. /30
3. /28
4. /29

Correct Answer(s): 2

Explanation:

An IPv4 address consists of 32 bits. The first x number of bits in the address is the network address and the remaining bits are used for the host addresses. The subnet mask defines how many bits form the network address and from that, we can calculate how many bits are used for the host addresses. In this question, the /30 subnet mask dictates that the first 30 bits of the IP address that are used for network addressing and the remaining 2 bits are used for host addressing. The formula to calculate the number of hosts in a subnet is 2n - 2. The "n" in the host's formula represents the number of bits used for host addressing. If we apply the formula (22 - 2), a /30 subnet mask will provide 2 usable IP addresses.

QUESTION 32:

A company wants to install a new wireless network. The network must be compatible with 802.11ac protocol in order to obtain the maximum amount of throughput available. Which of the following frequencies will this wireless network utilize?

1. 2.4GHz
2. 3.7GHz
3. 5.0GHz
4. 6.0GHz

Correct Answer(s): 3

Explanation:

Wireless AC uses 5.0 GHz for wireless transmission, whereas Wireless B/G uses 2.4 GHz.

QUESTION 33:

Patches have just been released by a third-party vendor to resolve a major vulnerability. There are over 100 critical devices that need to be updated. What action should be taken to ensure the patch is installed with minimal downtime?

1. Test the patch in a lab environment and then install it in the production network during the next scheduled maintenance
2. Download and install all patches in the production network during the next scheduled maintenance period
3. Configure endpoints to automatically download and install the patches
4. Deploy the patch in a lab environment, quickly conduct testing, and then immediately install it in the production environment

Correct Answer(s): 4

Explanation:

Patches should always be tested first. Once successfully tested, deployment to the production environment can then be accomplished.

QUESTION 34:

A network technician discovers an issue with spanning tree on the core switch. Which step should the network technician perform NEXT when troubleshooting to resolve the issue?

1. Test a theory to determine the cause
2. Escalate to a senior technician
3. Identify the symptoms
4. Establish a theory of probable cause

Correct Answer(s): 4

Explanation:

If the technician has already discovered the issue, the symptoms have already been identified. Testing the theory comes after you have established a theory, which can only come once the issue has been discovered. Establishing a theory of probable cause allows you to continue with the next steps in troubleshooting the issue.

QUESTION 35:

You have just finished installing a small network consisting of a router, a firewall, and a single computer. What type of physical network topology have you created in this scenario?

1. Ring
2. Bus
3. Mesh
4. Star

Correct Answer(s): 2

Explanation:

As described, this network would resemble a physical bus network topology because the firewall connects directly to the router, and the router connects directly to the computer. This would form a single line (or bus) from one device to the next.

QUESTION 36:

Janet is a system administrator who is troubleshooting an issue with a DNS server. She notices that the security logs have filled up and that they need to be cleared from the event viewer. She recalls this being a daily occurrence. Which of the following would BEST resolve this issue?

1. Increase the maximum log size
2. Log into the DNS server every hour to check if the logs are full
3. Install an event management tool
4. Delete the logs when full

Correct Answer(s): 3

Explanation:

Using an event management tool will allow the administrator to clear the event logs and move them from the server to a centralized database, if needed.

QUESTION 37:

The Security Operations Center is trying to determine if there are any network anomalies currently being observed. To assist them, you gather information about the current performance of the network. Which of the following should you also gather to compare the current information against?

1. Logs
2. PCAP
3. NETFLOW
4. Baseline

Correct Answer(s): 4

Explanation:

While all of the network artifacts, such as Logs, PCAP, and NETFLOW data are useful, the general terms for the historical network performance data is a baseline. A baseline may be created from these other types of data, but based on the question, the BEST and most correct answer is a baseline.

QUESTION 38:

The RAID controller on a server failed and was replaced with a different brand. What will be needed after the server has been rebuilt and joined to the domain?

1. Vendor documentation

2. Recent backups
3. Physical IP address
4. Physical network diagram

Correct Answer(s): 2

Explanation:

If the RAID controller fails and is replaced with a RAID controller with a different brand, the RAID will break. We would have to rebuild a new RAID disk and access and restore the most recent backup to the new RAID disk.

QUESTION 39:

An administrator has a virtualization environment that includes a vSAN and iSCSI switching. Which of the following actions could the administrator take to improve the performance of data transfers over iSCSI switches?

1. The administrator should configure the switch ports to auto-negotiate the proper Ethernet settings.
2. The administrator should configure each vSAN participant to have its own VLAN.
3. The administrator should connect the iSCSI switches to each other over inter-switch links (ISL).
4. The administrator should set the MTU to 9000 on each of the participants in the vSAN.

Correct Answer(s): 4

Explanation:

When using an iSCSI SAN (with iSCSI switching), we can improve network performance by enabling 'jumbo frames'. A jumbo frame is a frame with an MTU of more than 1500. By setting the MTU to 9000, there will be fewer but larger frames going over the network. Enabling jumbo frames can improve network performance by making data transmissions more efficient.

QUESTION 40:

A company has a secondary datacenter in a remote location. The cable management and power management are handled by the data center staff, while the building's security is also handled by the datacenter staff with little oversight from the company. Which of the following should the technician do to follow the best practices?

1. Secure the patch panels
2. Ensure power monitoring is enabled

3. Ensure rack security

4. Secure the UPS units

Correct Answer(s): 3

Explanation:

By ensuring rack security such as locks, RFID card locks, and swing handles, the technician adds an extra layer of security to the servers which is a best practice.

QUESTION 41:

Which of the following connector types is used to terminate DS3 connections in a telecommunications facility?

1. 66 block
2. BNC
3. F-connector
4. RJ-11

Correct Answer(s): 2

Explanation:

Bayonet Neill-Concelman Connector (BNC connector) is a type of coaxial RF (Radio frequency) electrical connector that is used in place of coaxial connectors. A DS3 (Digital Signal 3) is also known as a T3 line with a maximum bandwidth of 44.736 Mbit/s. DS3 uses 75 ohm coaxial cable and BNC connectors.

QUESTION 42:

Dion Training is trying to connect two geographically dispersed offices using a VPN connection. You have been asked to configure their networks to allow VPN traffic into the network. Which device should you configure FIRST?

1. Switch
2. Modem
3. Firewall
4. Router

Correct Answer(s): 3

Explanation:

You should FIRST configure the firewall, since the firewall is installed at the external boundary (perimeter) of the network. By allowing the VPN connection through the firewall, the two networks can be connected together and function as a single intranet (internal network).

QUESTION 43:

Dion Training has created a guest wireless network for students to use during class. This guest network is separated from the corporate network for security. Which of the following should be implemented to require the least amount of configuration for a student to be able to access the Internet over the guest network?

1. Enable SSID broadcast for the guest wireless network
2. Enable two-factor authentication on the student's device
3. Configure the access point to 802.1x for authentication
4. Configure WEP with a pre-shared key

Correct Answer(s): 1

Explanation:

Since security was not listed as a requirement for the guest wireless network, it would be easiest to not setup any encryption, passwords, or authentication mechanisms on the network. Instead, you should simply enable the SSID broadcast for the guest network so students can easily find and connect to it.

QUESTION 44:

What would provide the highest level of physical security for the client if they are concerned with theft of equipment from the datacenter?

1. Cipher lock
2. Proximity reader
3. Magnetic key swipe
4. Man trap

Correct Answer(s): 4

Explanation:

A man trap will ensure that only a single authorized person can get in or out of the building at one time. It provides the highest level of physical security among the choices given.

QUESTION 45:

The administrator's network has OSPF for the internal routing protocol. One port going out to the Internet is congested. The data is going out to the Internet, but queues up before sending. What would resolve this issue? Output: Fast Ethernet 0 is up, line protocol is up Int ip address is 10.20.130.5/25 MTU 1500 bytes, BW 10000 kbit, DLY 100 usec Reliability 255/255, Tx load 1/255, Rx load 1/255 Encapsulation ospf, loopback not set Keep alive 10 Half duplex, 100Mb/s, 100 Base Tx/Fx Received 1052993 broadcasts 0 input errors 983881 packets output, 768588 bytes 0 output errors, 0 collisions, 0 resets

1. Set the loopback address
2. Change the IP address
3. Change the slash notation
4. Change duplex to full

Correct Answer(s): 4

Explanation:

From the output, we see that the half-duplex is configured. This would not use the full capacity of ports on the network. By changing to full duplex, the throughput would be doubled.

QUESTION 46:

Your company wants to develop a voice solution to provide 23 simultaneous connections using VoIP. Which of the following technologies could BEST provide this capability?

1. DOCSIS
2. T1
3. DSL
4. POTS

Correct Answer(s): 2

Explanation:

A T1 can transmit 24 telephone calls at a time because it uses a digital carrier signal (DS-1). DS-1 is a communications protocol for multiplexing the bit streams of up to 24 telephone calls simultaneously. The T1's maximum data transmission rate is 1.544 mbps. DOCSIS is the standard for a cable modem. DSL is a Digital Subscriber Line which has variable speeds from 256 kbps and up. POTS is the Plain Old Telephone System, and provides only a single phone connection at a time. Out of these options, the T1 is the BEST to ensure you can reliably provide 23 simultaneous phone connections.

QUESTION 47:

A network technician needs to install a server to authenticate remote users before they have access to corporate network resources when working from home. Which kind of server should the network technician implement?

1. DNSSEC
2. PPP
3. RAS
4. VLAN

Correct Answer(s): 3

Explanation:

A remote access server is a type of server that provides a suite of services to remotely connect users to a network or the Internet. Usually this will be a RDP or VNC server.

QUESTION 48:

Your company is using a T1 connection for its connectivity to the internet. When you arrived at work this morning, you found that your internet connection was not working properly. You began troubleshooting and verified that the network's router is properly configured, the cable is connected properly between the router and the T1's CSU/DSU, but the T1 remains down. You call your ISP and they have requested that you test the interface on the CSU/DSU to ensure it hasn't failed. Which tool should you utilize to perform this test?

1. Cable tester
2. Tone generator
3. Light meter
4. Loopback adapter

Correct Answer(s): 4

Explanation:

If you have a T1 for internet service, it is highly recommended that you have a T1 loopback adapter or plug for testing purposes if the line ever has trouble on it. By inserting the loopback adapter into the CSU/DSU, this will allow the ISP to remotely diagnosis if the connection between their central office and your demarcation point is working properly.

QUESTION 49:

An administrator would like to test out an open-source based phone system prior to making an investment in hardware and phones. Which of the following should the administrator do to BEST test the software?

1. Create virtual IP phones that utilizes the STP protocol in your lab
2. Deploy an open-source VDI solution to create a testing lab
3. Deploy new SIP appliances and connect them to the open source phone applications
4. Create a virtual PBX and connect it to SIP phone applications

Correct Answer(s): 4

Explanation:

To test out the system prior to purchasing it, he should connect to a virtual PBX with a SIP phone application and ensure it meets his need. Deploying new SIP appliances would be costly, therefore a bad choice. Deploying a VDI is a virtual desktop infrastructure solution, which doesn't have anything to do with phones. Creating virtual IP phones in a lab may work but isn't going to give him an accurate representation of the actual usage of the system.

QUESTION 50:

Which of the following would be the BEST addition to a business continuity plan to protect the business from a catastrophic disaster such as a fire, tornado, or earthquake?

1. UPS and battery backups
2. Fire suppression systems
3. Building generator
4. Hot sites or cold sites

Correct Answer(s): 4

Explanation:

Although all answers are adequate suggestions to aid in business continuity, the addition of a hot or cold site is the BEST option. A hot or cold site is a commercial service that provides all equipment and facilities to allow a computer or networking company to continue operations in the event of a catastrophic event. In the case that the building has been destroyed, the hot/cold site is the only option that will allow the business to continue their operations effectively.

QUESTION 51:

A technician has punched down only the middle two pins (pins 4 and 5) on an Ethernet patch panel. Which of the following has the technician cabled this port to be used with?

1. 10baseT
2. POTS
3. 568B
4. 568A

Correct Answer(s): 2

Explanation:

POTS is short for plain old telephone service. The technician was making a cable for a telephone to use, since it only requires two pins (send and receive).

QUESTION 52:

Your company has just hired a contractor to attempt to exploit a weakness in your network to identify all their vulnerabilities. This person has been giving permission to perform these actions and will only conduct their actions within the scope of work of their contract. Which of the following will be conducted by the contractor?

1. Vulnerability scanning
2. Hacktivism
3. Social engineering
4. Penetration testing

Correct Answer(s): 4

Explanation:

Penetration testing is the practice of testing a computer system, network, or web application to find security vulnerabilities that an attacker could exploit. Penetration testers only do this with permission of the organization who owns the system, network, or web application, and within the bounds of their scope of work. In vulnerability scanning, the person will not attempt to exploit a weakness. Social engineering may be used as part of a penetration test, but it does not adequately describe the scenario provided. Hacktivism is when someone is hacking an organization without permission based on their own set of morals and values.

QUESTION 53:

You are troubleshooting a wireless network. A user has complained that their iPad cannot connect to the wireless network from their desk in the corner of the office building. The user has no issues connecting to the wireless network with the tablet when they are located in the break room area at the center of the building. You measured the distance from their office to the 802.11 AC wireless access point, and it is about 170 feet. What is MOST likely the cause of the tablet not connecting to the WAP?

1. Refraction
2. Reflection
3. Distance
4. Absorption

Correct Answer(s): 3

Explanation:

A general rule of thumb in home networking says that Wifi routers operating on the traditional 2.4 GHz and 5.0 GHz bands can reach up to about 150 feet (46 m) indoors and 300 feet (92 m) outdoors. Since the distance is listed as 170 feet, the issue is likely caused by the user's office being too far from the WAP.

QUESTION 54:

A network technician is tasked with designing a firewall to improve security for an existing FTP server that is on the company network and is accessible from the Internet. Security personnel are concerned that the FTP server is compromised and is possibly being used as a platform to attack other company servers. What is the BEST way to mitigate this risk?

1. Add an outbound ACL to the firewall
2. Change the FTP server to a more secure SFTP
3. Use the implicit deny of the firewall
4. Move the server to the company's DMZ

Correct Answer(s): 4

Explanation:

The DMZ is the subnetwork of a network that hosts public-facing servers and has additional security added to it.

QUESTION 55:

An administrator notices an unused cable behind a cabinet that is terminated with a DB-9 connector. What protocol was MOST likely used on this cable?

1. RS-232
2. 802.3
3. ATM
4. Token Ring

Correct Answer(s): 1

Explanation:

RS-232 is a standard for serial communication transmission of data. It formally defines the signals connecting between a DTE (data terminal equipment) such as a computer terminal, and a DCE (data circuit-terminating equipment or data communication equipment).

QUESTION 56:

Which type of equipment should be used for telecommunications equipment and have an open design?

1. 2/4 post racks
2. Rail racks
3. Vertical frame
4. Ladder racks

Correct Answer(s): 1

Explanation:

The 2/4 post racks are open framed which are most common with telecommunication equipment.

QUESTION 57:

An outside technician notices that a SOHO employee who is logged into the company VPN has an unexpected source IP address. What is the employee MOST likely using?

1. Proxy server
2. Least-cost routing
3. IPv6
4. VPN concentrator

Correct Answer(s): 1

Explanation:

Proxy servers are just different computers that serve as a hub where Internet requests are processed. When you are connected to a proxy, your computer sends request to that server and then returns your answers to the proxy server before forwarding the data to the requesting computer.

QUESTION 58:

You are configuring a new machine with a hypervisor and several operating systems hosted within it that will be used for developing some new applications. You want to ensure that the various virtual machines hosted by the hypervisor can communicate with each other over a network, but you don't want their network traffic to leave the hypervisor itself. What is the BEST solution to meet these requirements?

1. Install and configure a virtual switch
2. Install and configure individual routes between the virtual machines
3. Configure each virtual machine to use a route to a default gateway
4. Connect each machine to an individual switch

Correct Answer(s): 1

Explanation:

A virtual switch is a software program that allows one virtual machine (VM) to communicate with another. This is usually created within the hypervisor's software.

QUESTION 59:

A NAC service has discovered a virus on a client laptop. What location should the NAC service put the laptop?

1. On the DMZ network
2. On the sandbox network
3. On the honeypot
4. On the quarantine network

Correct Answer(s): 4

Explanation:

Network Access Control (NAC) is an approach to computer security that attempts to unify endpoint security technology (such as antivirus, host intrusion prevention, and vulnerability assessment), user or system authentication, and network security enforcement. When NAC detects an issue with a client, it places them in a quarantine network.

QUESTION 60:

An additional network segment is urgently needed for QA testing on the external network. A software release could be impacted if this change is not immediate. The request come directly from management, and there is no time to go through the emergency change management process. Which of the following should the technician do?

1. Wait until the maintenance window and make the requested change
2. First document the potential impacts and procedures related to the change
3. Send out a notification to the company about the change
4. Make the change, document the requester, and document all network changes

Correct Answer(s): 4

Explanation:

While this is a difficult situation, the best answer is to make the change, document the requester, and document all the network changes. Since the request came directly from management, if they have sufficient authority to authorize the change, it can be performed outside of the emergency change control process. This should be a RARE occurrence.

QUESTION 61:

The network administrator is troubleshooting a switch port for a file server with dual NICs. The file server needs to be configured for redundancy and the dual NICs needs to be combined for maximum throughput. What feature on the switch should the network administrator ensure is enabled for best results?

1. BPDU
2. LACP
3. Spanning tree
4. Load balancing

Correct Answer(s): 2

Explanation:

LACP is a protocol used to control the combining of ports. Link Aggregation groups combine numerous physical ports to make one high bandwidth path. This method can increase bandwidth and therefore, throughput. It can also provide network redundancy and load balancing.

QUESTION 62:

Jason wants to use his personal cell phone for work-related purposes. Because of his position in the company, Jason has access to sensitive company data which might be stored on his cell phone during its usage. The company is concerned about this but believes with the proper security controls in place it might be acceptable. Which of the following should be done to protect both the company and Jason if they allow him to use his personal cell phone for work-related purposes?

1. Establish a consent to monitoring policy so that the company can audit Jason's cell phone usage
2. Establish a AUP that allows a personal phone to be used for work-related purposes
3. Conduct real-time monitoring of the phone's activity and usage
4. Establish an NDA that states Jason cannot share the confidential data with others

Correct Answer(s): 3

Explanation:

While all four are good options, the BEST solution is to conduct real-time monitoring of the phone's activity since it is a technical control that could identify an issue quickly. The other options are all administrative controls (policies), which are useful, but would not actually identify if the sensitive data was leaked from Jason's phone.

QUESTION 63:

A company has added a lot of new users to the network that is causing an increase in network traffic by 200%. Original projection by the engineers was that the new users would only add 20-30% more network traffic, not 200%. The network administrator suspects that a compromise of the network may have occurred. What should the network administrator have done previously to prevent this network breach?

1. Create VLANs to segment the network traffic
2. Place a network sniffer on segments with new employees
3. Provide end user awareness and training for employees
4. Ensure best practices were implemented when creating new user accounts

Correct Answer(s): 3

Explanation:

With new employees entering a company, often they are not fully aware of the company's Internet usage policy and safe Internet practices. Providing end user awareness and training for new employees help reduce the company's vulnerability to malicious entities on the Internet.

QUESTION 64:

A system administrator wants to verify that external IP addresses are unable to collect software versioning from servers on the network. Which of the following should the system administrator do to confirm the network is protected?

1. Analyze packet captures
2. Utilize netstat to locate active connections
3. Use nmap to query known ports
4. Review the ID3 logs on the network

Correct Answer(s): 1

Explanation:

Captured packets show you the information that was travelling through certain files, etc. Packet sniffers detail the information they've received, so working through those would show if the external network shows or details software versions.

QUESTION 65:

You work for a fast food restaurant which is installing a new electronic sign board to display their menu items to customers. The signboard is connected to the network and it came preconfigured with a public IP address so that the central office can connect to it remotely to update the menu items and prices being displayed. This new signboard was installed by one of the other employees who simply unboxed the new device, hung it on the wall, and plugged it into the network. When you arrive at work the next day, you see that the menu items have all been changed to include vulgar names and prices like $6.66. It appears the signboard has been hacked and is being used for digital vandalism. What is the MOST likely reason the attackers were able to access the signboard?

1. The signboard's self-signed digital certificate had expired
2. Unnecessary services were not disabled on the signboard during installation
3. The signboard default ports were left open

4. The signboard's default credentials were never changed during installation

Correct Answer(s): 4

Explanation:

Since the signboard was installed with all the defaults still in place (since the employee who installed it simply removed it from the box, hung it on the wall, and plugged it in), it is most likely that the electronic signboard default credentials were never changed. While the other options may cause an issue, the unchanged default username and passwords are the biggest threat and most likely cause of the hack/vandalism act.

QUESTION 66:

Sally in the web development group has asked for your assistance in troubleshooting her latest website. When she attempts to connect to the web server as a user, her web browser issues a standard HTTP request, but continually receives a timeout response in return. You decided that to best troubleshoot the issue, you should capture the entire TCP handshake between her workstation and the web server. Which of the following tools would BEST allow you to capture and then analyze the TCP handshake?

1. Protocol analyzer
2. Packet sniffer
3. Spectrum analyzer
4. Tone generator

Correct Answer(s): 1

Explanation:

A protocol analyzer or packet analyzer (like Wireshark) has the capability to capture the handshake and display it for analysis. A packet sniffer, though, will only capture the handshake. Neither a spectrum analyzer or a tone generator would be helpful in this situation.

QUESTION 67:

The network administrator noticed that the border router is having high network capacity loading during non-working hours. This load is causing web services outages. Which of the following is the MOST likely cause of the issue?

1. Evil twin
2. Session hijacking

3. Distributed DoS
4. ARP cache poisoning

Correct Answer(s): 3

Explanation:

Distributed Denial of Service (DDoS) is when a computer or multiple computers are compromised due to a network breach or virus attack. This kind of attack can impact the network and cause outages or slowness, if your workstation is affected and acting as part of a botnet.

QUESTION 68:

A company is implementing enhanced user authentication for system administrators accessing the company's confidential servers. They intend to use two-factor authentication to accomplish this. Which of these BEST represents two-factor authentication?

1. ID badge and keys
2. Password and key fob
3. Fingerprint scanner and retina scan
4. Username and password

Correct Answer(s): 2

Explanation:

Two–factor authentication requires 2 out of 3 of the following: something you know, something you have, something you are. The only correct answer therefore is Password (something you know) and key fob (something you have).

QUESTION 69:

Which of the following provides accounting, authorization, and authentication via a centralized privileged database, as well as challenge/response and password encryption?

1. Multi-factor authentication
2. ISAKMP
3. TACACS+
4. Network access control

Correct Answer(s): 3

Explanation:

TACACS+ is a AAA (accounting, authorization, and authentication) protocol to provide AAA services for access to routers, network access points, and other networking devices.

QUESTION 70:

A user reports slow computer performance. A technician troubleshooting the issue uses a performance monitoring tool and receives the following results: Avg % Processor Time =10% Avg Pages/Second = 0 Avg Disk Queue Length = 3 Based on the results, what might be causing a bottleneck in performance?

1. Hard drive
2. Memory
3. Processor
4. NIC

Correct Answer(s): 1

Explanation:

Based on the results, the hard drive (disk queue) is causing the bottle neck. Since the average processor is not over 50%, the pages/second (memory) is not heavily burdened, nor do we have any information on the NIC.

QUESTION 71:

You have just received an email regarding a security issue that was detected on the company's standard web browser. Which of the following should you do to fix the issue?

1. Firmware update
2. OS update
3. Vulnerability patch
4. Driver update

Correct Answer(s): 3

Explanation:

Since there is a security issue with the current web browser, it most likely needs to be updated with a vulnerability patch from the manufacturer. A vulnerability patch is a piece of software that fixes security issues.

QUESTION 72:

Which network element enables unified communication devices to connect to and traverse traffic onto the PSTN?

1. Access switch
2. UC gateway
3. UC server
4. Edge router

Correct Answer(s): 2

Explanation:

Unified Communications (UC) enables people using different modes of communication, different media, and different devices to communicate with anyone, anywhere, at any time. To accomplish this, a UC gateway is needed.

QUESTION 73:

A technician is troubleshooting an area that is having difficulty connecting to a WAP. After identifying the symptoms, what should the technician do NEXT?

1. Document findings
2. Resolve the issue
3. Establish the probable cause
4. Implement a solution

Correct Answer(s): 3

Explanation:

Establishing the probable cause is the second step in the troubleshooting process, which allows the technician to list reasons from top to bottom, beginning with the simplest and most obvious issues to the most complex.

QUESTION 74:

Which of the following would require the network administrator to schedule a maintenance window?

1. When a company-wide email notification must be sent
2. A minor release upgrade of a production router
3. When the network administrator's laptop must be rebooted
4. A major release upgrade of a core switch in a test lab

Correct Answer(s): 2

Explanation:

During an update of a production router, the router would not be able to route packages and the network traffic would be affected. It would be necessary to announce a maintenance window. A maintenance window is a period of time designated in advance by the technical staff, during which preventive maintenance that could cause disruption of service may be performed.

QUESTION 75:

Workers in a company branch office are required to visit an initial web page and click the "I agree" button prior to being able to surf the web. Which of the following is this an example of?

1. An end-user license agreement
2. An SLA
3. An AUP
4. An MOU

Correct Answer(s): 3

Explanation:

AUP stands for acceptable use policy. If you're agreeing to what you can and can't view, you're agreeing to the policy. MOU is memo of understanding which typically contains an agreement on certain actions. SLA is service-level agreement which is usually made between two companies to state what level of service is expected if machines go down, etc., and when they can expect to be back up and running.

Practice Exam #4

QUESTION 1:

You are installing a Small Office/Home Office (SOHO) network consisting of a router with 2 ports, a switch with 8 ports, and a hub with 4 ports. The router has one port connected to a cable modem and one port connected to switch port #1. The hub's first port is connected to switch port #2. Based on the description provided, how many collision domains exist in this network?

1. 8
2. 11
3. 3
4. 9

Correct Answer(s): 4

Explanation:

Based on the description provided, there are 9 collision domains. Each port on the router is a collision domain (2), each port on the switch is a collision domain (8), and all of the ports on the hub make up a single collision domain (1). But, since one of the ports on the router is connected to one of the ports on the switch, they are in the same collision domain (-1). Similarly, the hub and the switch share a common collision domain with their connection to each other over the switch port (-1). This gives us 9 collision domains total: the 8 ports on the switch, and the 1 port on the route that is used by the cable modem.

QUESTION 2:

Your company hosts all of the company's virtual servers internally in your own datacenter. In the event of total failure or disaster, though, the server images can be restored on a cloud provider and accessed through a VPN. Which of the following types of cloud services is your company using in this scenario?

1. Public IaaS
2. Hybrid SaaS
3. Community PaaS
4. Private SaaS

Correct Answer(s): 1

Explanation:

Infrastructure as a Service (IaaS) is the foundation of cloud computing. Rather than purchasing or leasing space in expensive datacenter, labor, real estate, and all of the utilities to maintain and deploy computer servers, cloud networks, and storage, cloud buyers rent space in a virtual data center from an IaaS provider. They have access to the virtual data center via the Internet. This type of cloud computing provides the "raw materials" for IT, and users usually only pay for the resources they consume, including (but not limited to) CPU cores, RAM, hard disk or storage space, and data transfer. Since this cloud provider is available to all companies to use, much like Microsoft Azure or Amazon Web Services, this is an example of a Public IaaS or Public Cloud.

QUESTION 3:

Which of the following should be implemented to allow wireless network access for clients in the lobby using a password key?

1. RADIUS
2. IPSec
3. Firewall
4. WPA2

Correct Answer(s): 4

Explanation:

WPA2 allows the use of a preshared key for wireless network access.

QUESTION 4:

A company is experiencing accessibility issues reaching services on a cloud-based system. What monitoring tools should be used to locate possible outages?

1. Protocol analyzer
2. Network sniffer
3. Network analyzer
4. Packet analyzer

Correct Answer(s): 3

Explanation:

A network analyzer is a useful tool, helping you do things like track traffic and malicious usage on the network. A software tool like Wireshark is a network analyzer and protocol analyzer.

QUESTION 5:

You have been asked by the physical security manager to assist with his risk assessment of his proposed security measures. He is concerned that during a power outage, the server room might be the target of an attack. Luckily, he has many different protection measures in place to keep intruders out of the server room. During a power outage, which of the following security controls would still be usable?

1. Motion detectors
2. Biometric scanners
3. CCTV
4. Door locks

Correct Answer(s): 4

Explanation:

A traditional door lock doesn't require power to operate, therefore it will still provide protection to the keep the intruder out of the server room. The other options all require power to function and operate.

QUESTION 6:

Thomas has a server that streams media to the local network and the device is currently visible on the network. All of the workstations on the LAN can ping the device and all the firewalls are currently turned off. The goal is for the streaming media server to be able to allow different workstations to watch the stream if they choose to subscribe to it.The streaming device appears to be functioning properly, but the media won't stream when requested. Which of the following TCP/IP technologies is MOST likely not implemented properly?

1. Multicast
2. Unicast
3. Anycast
4. Broadcasts

Correct Answer(s): 1

Explanation:

Multicast is not implemented properly because that is the TCP/IP technology that sends out the packets to the requested devices when streaming to multiple workstations from a single streaming media server. As opposed to broadcast (one-to-all), which sends out packets to all devices, multicast (one-to-many-of-many/many-to-many-of-many) only sends packets to many that are specifically requested but not all. Multicast would need to be implemented to route the network device to the LAN so that streaming can function properly.

QUESTION 7:

A network architect is designing a highly-redundant network with a distance vector routing protocol in order to prevent routing loops. The architect has configured the routers to advertise failed routes with the addition of an infinite metric. What method should the architect utilize?

1. Route poisoning
2. Spanning tree
3. Hold down timers
4. Split horizon

Correct Answer(s): 1

Explanation:

The Route poisoning setting in Cisco's Split Horizon is what prevents routing loops and shows the failed routes.

QUESTION 8:

A network technician receives the following alert from a network device: "High utilizations threshold exceeded on gi1/0/24 : current value 8463257.54" What is being monitored to trigger the alarm?

1. Speed and duplex mismatch
2. Interface link status
3. Network device CPU
4. Network device memory

Correct Answer(s): 2

Explanation:

This is an error message that indicates that threshold of high utilization of network interface, in this case interface gi1/0/24, has been exceeded. The message has been triggered on the interface link status. (Note: gi1/0 would be a gigabyte interface.)

QUESTION 9:

You are working for a brand new startup company who allows you to use your own laptop, tablet, or other devices while at work. The company does provide some rules and guidelines that you must follow based on their policy. Which of the following policies should you look at to ensure you understand these rules and guidelines?

1. BYOD
2. NDA
3. MOU
4. SOP

Correct Answer(s): 1

Explanation:

BYOD (Bring Your Own Device) refers to the policy of permitting employees to bring personally owned devices to their workplace, and to use those devices to access privileged company information and applications.

QUESTION 10:

Which network device operates at Layer 2?

1. Firewall
2. Router
3. Repeater
4. Switch

Correct Answer(s): 4

Explanation:

A basic switch operates at Layer 2 of the OSI model. For the exam, unless they mention a "multilayer switch" or "layer 3 switch", always assume they are referencing a basic layer 2 switch.

QUESTION 11:

A network technician has received reports of an Internet-based application that has stopped functioning. Employees reported that after updating the Internet browsers, the application began to fail. Many users rolled back the update, but this did not correct the issue. Which of the following should the company do to reduce this type of action from causing network problems in the future?

1. Verify the update hashes match those on the vendor's website
2. Segment the network and create a test lab for all updates before deployment
3. Coordinate the Internet Server update to coincide with the users' updates
4. Implement a disaster recovery plan with a hot site to allow users to continue working

Correct Answer(s): 2

Explanation:

Segmented networks would ensure every system isn't updated at the same time and would be updated in groups. The test lab would ensure proper functionality prior to deployment or would allow you to work through the technical difficulties prior to deployment.

QUESTION 12:

A network technician needs to protect IP-based servers in the network DMZ from an intruder trying to discover them. What should the network technician do to protect the network from ping sweeps?

1. Disable TCP/IP on the server
2. Block ICMP at the firewall
3. Block echo replies inbound to the DMZ
4. Disable UDP on the servers

Correct Answer(s): 2

Explanation:

All ping requests are based on Internet Control Message Protocol. Blocking ICMP communication at the firewall would stop the firewall from communicating with any ping sweeps that would occur.

QUESTION 13:

An administrator has configured a new 100Mbps WAN circuit, but speed testing shows poor performance when downloading larger files. The download initially reaches close to 100Mbps but begins to drop and show spikes in the download speeds over time. The administrator checks the router interface and sees the following:

NETRTR01# show interface eth 1/1 GigabitEthernet 1/1 is up, line is up

Hardware is GigabitEthernet, address is 000F.33CC.F13AConfigured speed auto, actual 1Gbit, configured duplex fdx, actual fdx

Member of L2 VLAN 1, port is untagged, port state is forwarding

What is the issue?

1. Reset the statistics counter for this interface
2. Shutdown and restart the router
3. Remove default 802.1q tag and set to server VLAN
4. Shutdown and then re-enable this interface

Correct Answer(s): 3

Explanation:

Since the VLAN port is untagged, it can be slowing down performance. It is recommended to remove the default VLAN tag and setup a server VLAN to increase performance.

QUESTION 14:

As you arrive to work this morning, you look up at the building and notice a microwave antenna that is pointing another antenna on top of your company's support building across the street. Which of the following network topologies BEST represents this network connection over the microwave link?

1. Peer-to-Peer
2. Point-to-Multipoint
3. Mesh
4. Point-to-Point

Correct Answer(s): 4

Explanation:

This connection is best represented by a point-to-point connection since it is being used as a Campus Area Network connection to directly connect the two buildings.

QUESTION 15:

Your company is experiencing slow network speeds of about 54Mbps on their wireless network. You have been asked to perform an assessment on the existing wireless network and recommend a solution. You have recommended that the company upgrade to a 802.11n or 802.11ac wireless infrastructure to obtain higher network speeds. Which of the following technologies allows an 802.11n or 802.11ac network to achieve faster speeds?

1. PoE
2. MIMO
3. LWAPP
4. WPA2

Correct Answer(s): 2

Explanation:

One way 802.11n and 802.11ac networks achieve superior throughput and speeds is by using a technology called multiple input, multiple output (MIMO). MIMO uses multiple antennas for transmission and reception, which in turn results in higher speeds than 802.11a and 802.11g networks which can only support up to 54 mbps of throughput.

QUESTION 16:

(This is a simulated Performance-Based Question.)

The company's corporate headquarters provided your branch office a portion of their Class C subnet to use at a new office location. You must allocate the minimum number of addresses using CIDR notation in order to accommodate each department's needs.

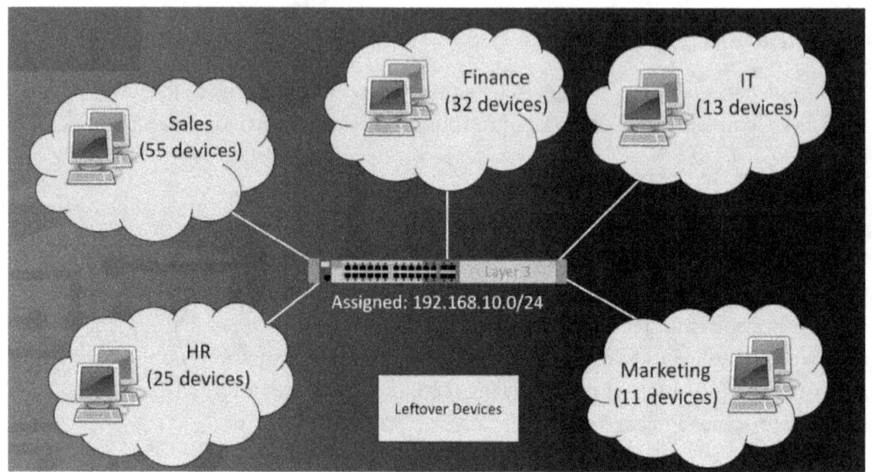

What is the correct CIDR notation for the Information Technology (IT) department's subnet which requires 13 devices?

1. /25
2. /28
3. /29
4. /27
5. /26
6. /30

Correct Answer(s): 2

Explanation:

Since the IT department needs 13 devices plus a network ID and broadcast IP, it will require 15 IP addresses. The smallest subnet that can fit 15 IPs is a /28 (16 IPs).

QUESTION 17:

Which of the following describes a design where traffic is shared between multiple network servers to provide greater throughput and reliability?

1. Multiplexing
2. Load balancing
3. VLAN tagging
4. MPLS trunking

Correct Answer(s): 2

Explanation:

Load Balancing is a technique used to spread work across multiple computers, network links, or other devices.

QUESTION 18:

A network administrator has set up a firewall and entered only three rules allowing network traffic over ports 21, 110, and 25 in an effort to minimize the attack surface and to better secure the network. Unfortunately, now the administrator is receiving complaints from users who are reporting that they cannot access any web pages using their URLs, such as DionTraining.com. Which of the following should the administrator do to correct this issue?

1. Add a rule to the ACL to allow traffic on ports 143 and 22
2. Add a rule to the ACL to allow traffic on ports 445 and 173
3. Add a rule to the ACL to allow traffic on ports 137 and 66
4. Add a rule to the ACL to allow traffic on ports 80 and 53

Correct Answer(s): 4

Explanation:

Port 80 is used for HTTP traffic. It must be open to allow the web browser to make a request from the network to the web server. Port 53 is needed to reach the DNS servers in order to determine the IP address for a given URL or domain name (such resolving DionTraining.com to its IP address).

QUESTION 19:

The corporate network uses a centralized server to manage credentials for all of its network devices. What type of server is MOST likely being used in this configuration?

1. FTP
2. RADIUS
3. Kerberos
4. DNS

Correct Answer(s): 2

Explanation:

RADIUS is used to centrally manage credentials for network devices. TACACS is an older username and login system that uses authentication to determine access, while RADIUS combines authorization AND authentication. For this question, either RADIUS or TACACS would be an acceptable answer.

QUESTION 20:

Which of the following wireless characteristic does channel bonding improve?

1. Coverage area
2. Connection speed
3. Signal strength
4. Encryption strength

Correct Answer(s): 2

Explanation:

Channel Bonding is used to reduce redundancy or increase throughput, directly affecting the connection speed of a wireless connection. Signal strength only refers to the maximum transmitted power by an antenna.

QUESTION 21:

Which of the following devices does a CSU/DSU connect?

1. A T1 line to a network router
2. A local network to a VPN
3. A cable modem to a wireless router
4. An analog line to a network router

Correct Answer(s): 1

Explanation:

A CSU/DSU device is designed to connect a terminal device to a T1 line. The terminal device or Data Terminal Equipment (DTE) such as a router will connect to the T1 line via CSU/DSU (Channel Service Unit/Data Service Unit).

QUESTION 22:

A network technician has configured a point-to-point interface on a router. Once the fiber optic cables have been run, though, the interface will not come up. The technician has cleaned the fiber connectors and used an optical power meter to confirm that light is passing in both directions without excessive loss. What is the MOST likely cause of this issue?

1. Distance limitation
2. Cross-talk
3. Wavelength mismatch
4. EMI

Correct Answer(s): 3

Explanation:

Wavelength mismatch is when one or more wavelengths in a fiber optic cable are unequal and cannot be measured using an optical power meter. Cross-talk and EMI are both elements that are irrelevant to Fiber optics.

QUESTION 23:

You are currently working as a firewall technician. You have received a request to open up a few ports on the firewall to allow a newly VoIP system to operate properly. The installer has requested that the ports associated with SIP, RDP, H.323, and RTP be opened to allow the new system to operate properly. Which of these ports are NOT used by a typical VoIP system?

1. H.323
2. SIP
3. RDP
4. RTP

Correct Answer(s): 3

Explanation:

RDP is the protocol for the Remote Desktop Protocol and operates over port 3389. This is not used in a typical VoIP system. SIP (Session Initiation Protocol), H.323 (voice/video conferencing) protocol, and the RTP (Real-time Transport Protocol) are all used heavily in VoIP and video conferencing solutions.

QUESTION 24:

What anti-malware solution should be implemented to deter attackers from loading custom files onto a distributed target platform?

1. Network-based anti-malware
2. Host-based anti-malware
3. Signature-based anti-malware
4. Cloud-based anti-malware

Correct Answer(s): 1

Explanation:

The network-based anti-malware can keep the system secure by testing all communications to/from a distributed target platform.

QUESTION 25:

Your co-worker has just installed an unmanaged 24-port switch. He is concerned with the amount of broadcast traffic that may exist when using this device. How many broadcast domains are created when using this single 24-port switch?

1. 1
2. 24
3. 0
4. 2

Correct Answer(s): 1

Explanation:

A single 24-port unmanaged switch will have only 1 broadcast domains. Broadcast domains are split up by routers and VLANs. Since this is an unmanaged switch, it will only have a single broadcast domain, but it will have 24 collision domains.

QUESTION 26:

A technician wants to update the organization's disaster recovery plans. Which of the following would allow network devices to be replaced quickly in the event of a device failure?

1. Archives/backups
2. Vendor documentation
3. Proper asset tagging and labeling
4. Network Baseline

Correct Answer(s): 1

Explanation:

Having backups of the server data would allow for a quick recovery in the event of a device failure.

QUESTION 27:

(This is a simulated Performance-Based Question.) What is the correct color scheme for Pin 1 to Pin 8 for a T-568A connector?

1. white/orange, orange, white/green, blue, white/blue, green, white/brown, brown
2. blue, white/blue, orange, white/brown, brown, white/green, green, orange/white
3. white/green, green, white/orange, orange, blue, white/blue, white/brown, brown
4. white/green, green, orange/white, blue, white/blue, orange, white/brown, brown

Correct Answer(s): 4

Explanation:

You need to have the T-568-A and T-568-B standards memorized before test day, because you may be asked to perform a drag and drop exercise of placing the right colored wires into the right pin numbers based on a T-568A or T-568B connector. Remember, a straight through cable will have T-568B one both ends. If you are asked to make a cross-over cable, you need a T-568A on one side and a T-568B on the other side.

QUESTION 28:

You are assisting a member of your organization's security team during an incident response. The team member asks you to determine if there are any strange TCP connections occurring on a given workstation. You open the command prompt on the workstation. Which of the following tools would provide you with information on any TCP connections that currently exist on the workstation?

1. arp
2. tracert
3. netstat
4. route

Correct Answer(s): 3

Explanation:

Netstat (network statistics) is a command-line network utility tool that displays network connections for the Transmission Control Protocol (both incoming and outgoing), routing tables, and a number of network interface and network protocol statistics. It is useful when trying to determine if a workstation is attempting outbound connections due to malware (beaconing activity), or has ports open and listening for inbound connections.

QUESTION 29:

You have been hired by a company to upgrade their aging network. The network currently uses static routing for the internal network, but the organization wants to reconfigure it to use a dynamic routing protocol. The new dynamic routing protocol must support IPv4 and VLSM, at a minimum. Based on the requirements provided, which of the following routing protocols should you enable and configure?

1. OSPF
2. VRRP
3. RIPv1
4. HSRP

Correct Answer(s): 1

Explanation:

Of the options provided, only OSPF supports IPv4 and VLSM (Variable Length Subnet Mask). The other protocols do not support VLSM. (Note: RIPv2 and above does in fact support VLSM.

QUESTION 30:

While installing new network equipment, a network administrator wants to add infrastructure to keep the cables organized in the environment. The administrator also needs cables to be easily removed or added due to the constantly changing environment. Which of the following should be added to the network's cable distribution plant to achieve this goal?

1. Cable ties
2. Hook and loop straps
3. Raised floor
4. Ladder trays

Correct Answer(s): 4

Explanation:

Ladder trays are a cost-effective alternative and allow for easy installation of cables by electricians as well as future access for adding or removing cable runs.

QUESTION 31:

A wireless networking technician has completed a survey of a wireless network and documented the detected signal strengths in various locations. This document is known as ________________.

1. Network baseline
2. Bandwidth survey
3. Logical Network map
4. Heat map

Correct Answer(s): 4

Explanation:

A heat map will show the signal strengths of wireless network signals in various locations. Technicians will document this information and use it as a tool during troubleshooting and optimization efforts.

QUESTION 32:

A technician installs a new piece of hardware and now needs to add the device to the network management tool database. However, when adding the device to the tool using SNMP credentials, the tool cannot successfully interpret the results. Which of the following needs to be added to allow the network management tool to interpret the new device and control it using SNMP?

1. GET
2. WALK
3. TRAP
4. MIB

Correct Answer(s): 4

Explanation:

Management Information Base (MIB) is used for managing all entities on a network using Simple Network Management Protocol. It would allow whatever tool to correctly interpret the information received.

QUESTION 33:

Which encryption type MOST likely is used for securing the key exchange during a client-to-server VPN connection?

1. Kerberos
2. TKIP
3. AES
4. ISAKMP

Correct Answer(s): 4

Explanation:

ISAKMP is used in IPSec, which is commonly used in securing the key exchange during the establishment of a client-to-server VPN connection.

QUESTION 34:

A technician needs to limit the amount of broadcast traffic on a network and allow different segments to communicate with each other. Which of the following should the technician install to satisfy this requirement?

1. Add a multilayer switch and create a VLAN
2. Add a router and enable OSPF
3. Add a firewall and implement proper ACL
4. Add a bridge between two switches

Correct Answer(s): 1

Explanation:

By adding a multilayer (layer 3) switch, the technician can improve network routing performance and reduce broadcast traffic. Creating a VLAN provides LAN segmentation, as well, within the network and the multilayer switch can conduct the routing between VLANs as needed.

QUESTION 35:

(This is a simulated Performance-Based Question.)

Console Port

What type of cable would you use to connect to a console port?

1. Crossover
2. RG-6
3. Straight-through
4. Rollover

Correct Answer(s): 4

Explanation:

Typically, a router or switch's console port is connected using a rollover cable, which has an RS-232 (DB-9) port on one side and an RJ-45 on the other. If this was a real question on the exam, you would have the words provided in a list, and you would drag them below the appropriate drawing.

QUESTION 36:

On which type of cable is an F-connector is used?

1. RG6
2. SMF
3. Cat 5
4. MMF

Correct Answer(s): 1

Explanation:

An F connector is a coaxial RF connector commonly used for cable television with an RG6 cable. RG6 is a type of coaxial cable used to transmit audio and video signals to devices such as television sets.

QUESTION 37:

Which WAN technology relies on virtual circuits and point-to-multipoint connections?

1. PRI
2. Frame relay
3. MPLS
4. ISDN

Correct Answer(s): 2

Explanation:

Frame Relay is a WAN technology that specifies the physical and data link layers of digital telecommunications channels using a packet switching methodology. It supports the use of virtual circuits and point-to-multipoint connections. It is commonly used to connect multiple smaller corporate office locations back to a larger centralized headquarters.

QUESTION 38:

A company has implemented the capability to send all log files to a central location by utilizing an encrypted channel. The log files are sent to this location in order to be reviewed. A recent exploit has caused the company's encryption to become unsecure. What would be required to resolve the exploit?

1. Install recommended updates
2. Configure the firewall to block port 22
3. Send all log files through SMTP
4. Utilize an FTP service

Correct Answer(s): 1

Explanation:

If the encryption is insecure, then we must look for encryption software updates or patches. If they are available, we must install them.

QUESTION 39:

A network technician needs to identify active services that should be disabled on the network. What tool would BEST accomplish this?

1. Interface monitoring tool
2. Packet analyzer

3.   Port scanner
4.   Content filter

Correct Answer(s): 3

Explanation:

Port Scanner will scan for what ports are open or closed enabling certain services or not. Such as if port 22 is open, that means Secure Shell service is enabled. Or if port 25 is open then the SMTP service is enabled.

QUESTION 40:

What should be considered when troubleshooting the coverage and signal strength of a 802.11n WLAN?

1.   Temperature
2.   Malware
3.   Building materials in the area
4.   Humidity

Correct Answer(s): 3

Explanation:

Some building materials are more dense than others. The denser the object, the more you will have a degradation of signal. For optimal signal, a LoS (Line of sight) of 25 feet or less is advised as well.

QUESTION 41:

You are troubleshooting your company's T-1 connection to your ISP. The ISP has asked you to place a loopback on the device which connects your T-1 line to their central office. Which of the following devices should you connect the loopback plug on?

1.   Channel service unit
2.   Channel remote module
3.   Fiber optic modem
4.   Digital subscriber line modem

Correct Answer(s): 1

Explanation:

The CSU/DSU terminates a T1 line at the customer's site. Therefore, the CSU (Channel Service Unit) should have the loopback plug attached to test the connection.

QUESTION 42:

You have been asked to run a cable between a drop ceiling and a standard ceiling and ensure it meets the fire safety requirements for your local government. The cable will be used to support a 10GBaseT network connection for up to 100 meters. Which of the following cables should you use to meet these requirements?

1. PVC Cat 5e
2. PVC Cat 6a
3. Plenum Cat 5e
4. Plenum Cat 6a

Correct Answer(s): 4

Explanation:

Cat6a can also support 10Gbps for up to 100 meters using 10GBaseT. Cat 5e can only support 1000BaseT (1 Gbps) connections. Since we are concerned with the fire safety rating of the cable, we should use a Plenum cable, not a PVC cable.

QUESTION 43:

A technician is configuring a computer lab at a school. The computers need to be able to communicate with each other, but students using the computers should not be able to access the Internet. What rule on the firewall should the technician configure to prevent student access to the Internet?

1. Block all LAN to LAN traffic
2. Block all WAN to LAN traffic
3. Block all LAN to WAN traffic
4. Block all WLAN to WAN traffic

Correct Answer(s): 3

Explanation:

By blocking all traffic from the LAN to WAN, it will prevent the students from accessing the Internet by blocking all requests to the Internet.

QUESTION 44:

You have been assigned to assist with the deployment of a new web-based application to your company's intranet. After installing the application, it was identified that the database server is becoming overloaded by the number of requests that the users create. The team lead has proposed adding a device between the web server and the database server to alleviate the issue. Which of the following is being implemented by adding this new device?

1. Implement clustering and NIC teaming on the database server
2. Conduct port sniffing and protocol analysis
3. Implement load balancing and provide high availability
4. Conduct content filtering and network analysis

Correct Answer(s): 3

Explanation:

The device being added is most likely a load balancer. By adding this device, it will allow the delivery team to install a series of database servers to handle the requests by dividing the incoming requests among the various servers. NIC teaming would be an action that occurs on the database server itself, it is not a separate device. The other options are focused on troubleshooting efforts, not increasing the capability or availability of the database server(s).

QUESTION 45:

A technician just completed a new external website and setup access rules in the firewall. After some testing, only users outside the internal network can reach the site. The website responds to a ping from the internal network and resolves the proper public address. What can the technician do to fix this issue while causing internal users to route to the website using an internal IP address?

1. Place the server in the DMZ
2. Implement a split horizon DNS
3. Configure NAT on the firewall
4. Adjust the proper internal ACL

Correct Answer(s): 2

Explanation:

Split Domain Name System (Split DNS) is an implementation in which separate DNS servers are provided for internal and external networks as a means of security and privacy management.

QUESTION 46:

An administrator's router with multiple interfaces uses OSPF. When looking at the router's status, it is discovered that one interface is not passing traffic. Given the information below, what would resolve this issue? Output: Fast Ethernet 0 is up, line protocol is down Int ip address is 10.20.130.5/25 MTU 1500 bytes, BW 10000 kbit, DLY 100 usec Reliability 255/255, Tx load 1/255, Rx load 1/255 Encapsulation ospf, loopback not set Keep alive 10 Full duplex, 100Mb/s, 100 Base Tx/Fx Received 1052993 broadcasts 0 input errors 0 packets output, 0 bytes 0 output errors, 0 collisions, 0 resets

1. Replace the line card
2. Set OSPF to area 0
3. Put the IP address in the right broadcast domain
4. Set the loopback address
5. Enable the connecting port

Correct Answer(s): 5

Explanation:

Since the line protocol is down, you will need to enable the connecting port to restore the connection.

QUESTION 47:

A company utilizes a patching server to regularly update its PCs. After the latest round of patching, all of the older PCs with non-gigabit Ethernet cards become disconnected from the network and now require a technician to fix the issue locally at each PC. What could be done to prevent this problem next time?

1. Throttle the connection speed of the patching server to match older PCs
2. Enable automatic rebooting of the PCs after patching is completed
3. Require the patching server to update the oldest PCs off hours
4. Disable automatic driver updates to PCs on the patching server

Correct Answer(s): 4

Explanation:

The most likely cause of this issue was a forced driver update being pushed from the update server to the older PCs, breaking their ability to use their network cards. It is best to disable automatic driver updates for PCs and have them tested first.

QUESTION 48:

A network technician is using telnet to connect to a router on a network that has been compromised. A new user and password has been added to the router with full rights. The technician is concerned that the regularly used administrator account has been compromised. After changing the password on all the networking devices, which of the following should the technician do to prevent the password from being sniffed on the network again?

1. Use SNMPv1 for all configurations involving the router
2. Copy all configurations to routers using TFTP for security
3. Ensure the password is 10 characters, containing letters and numbers
4. Only allow administrators to access routers using port 22

Correct Answer(s): 4

Explanation:

Port 22 uses SSH to authenticate a remote computer or user, or in this case, an administrator. Even if the router has been compromised, the new full rights user would not be able to access their new account without the SSH key, which could only be provided by a true administrator. Telnet uses port 23 and passes all information as unencrypted traffic on the network. Telnet should always be disabled for security reasons and SSH (which uses encryption) should be used instead.

QUESTION 49:

Which of the following WAN connection types might an Amplitude Modulation (AM) radio station have a detrimental effect on and cause interference?

1. SONET
2. Metro-Ethernet
3. Frame relay
4. DOCSIS

Correct Answer(s): 4

Explanation:

DOCSIS is how cable modems operate by sending radio frequency waves over coaxial cables. AM frequencies can interfere with DOCSIS. The other answers all rely on networks, such as fiber, which are immune to radio frequency interference.

QUESTION 50:

A network administrator is configuring a VLAN across multiple switches. The administrator wants to configure the VLAN once and have that configuration propagate to all of the switches in the network. Which of the following should the administrator do?

1. Configure the switches to utilize IGRP
2. Implement port bonding on the switches
3. Configure the switches to utilize VTP
4. Configure the switches to utilize STP

Correct Answer(s): 3

Explanation:

VLAN Trunking Protocol (VTP) shares VLAN information to all switches in a network.

QUESTION 51:

A technician is troubleshooting a newly-installed WAP that is sporadically dropping connections to devices on the network. Which of the following should the technician check FIRST during troubleshooting?

1. WAP placement
2. Encryption type
3. Bandwidth saturation
4. WAP SSID

Correct Answer(s): 1

Explanation:

For optimal network performance, the placement of the Wireless Access Point (WAP) guidelines should be taken into consideration to ensure that the building's construction doesn't cause interference with the wireless signals.

QUESTION 52:

(This is a simulated Performance-Based Question.) A customer's email service is not sending emails anymore. What is the correct order that you should follow to perform the troubleshooting steps?

1. Determine if any recent changes have been made to the server; Establish a theory of probable cause; Test the theory to determine

cause; Establish a plan of action to resolve the problem; Implement the solution; Verify full system functionality; Implement preventative measures; Document findings, actions, and outcomes

2. Determine if any recent changes have been made to the server; Document findings, actions, and outcomes; Establish a plan of action to resolve the problem; Test the theory to determine cause; Implement preventative measures; Implement the solution; Verify full system functionality; Establish a theory of probable cause

3. Implement the solution; Verify full system functionality; Establish a theory of probable cause; Determine if any recent changes have been made to the server; Document findings, actions, and outcomes; Establish a plan of action to resolve the problem; Test the theory to determine cause; Implement preventative measures

Correct Answer(s): 1

Explanation:

You must know the CompTIA troubleshooting steps in the right order for the exam. You will see numerous questions both in the multiple-choice and simulation sections on this topic. If you received this question on the real exam, it will appear as a "drag and drop" question with each of the steps making up a single box, and you need to put them into the correct order.

QUESTION 53:

A network engineer is conducting an assessment for a customer who wants to implement an 802.11ac wireless network. Before the engineer can estimate the number of WAPs needed, it is important to reference the ________________.

1. PoE requirements
2. Site survey
3. Network diagram
4. Network topology

Correct Answer(s): 2

Explanation:

Since it is a wireless network, a review of a site survey is necessary to determine any physical advantages and disadvantages. Network topology and Network diagrams can be created once the site survey is complete and the location of the access points is determined.

QUESTION 54:

(This is a simulated Performance-Based Question. On the real certification exam, you would be asked to drag-and-drop the correct encryption onto the APs.)

Your company has purchased a new building down the street for its executive suites. You have been asked to choose the BEST encryption for AP1, AP2, and AP3 in order to establish a wireless connection inside the main building for visitors to use. Your boss has stated that the internal wireless network in the main building is for visitors' use only and MUST NOT require the visitors to setup any special configuration on their devices in order to connect.

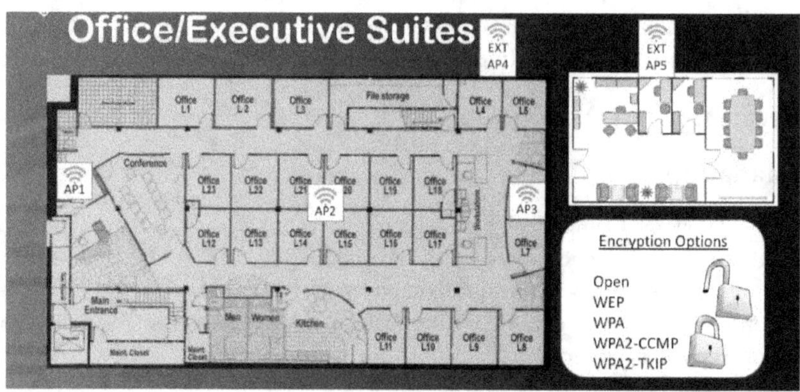

Which of the following is the BEST encryption to use from the options below to meet your manager's requirements for the new visitors' Wireless Network?

1. WPA2-TKIP
2. WEP
3. Open
4. WPA
5. WPA2-CCMP

Correct Answer(s): 3

Explanation:

Since your manager has requested that the visitors not be required to configure anything on their devices, the only option you can choose is Open. This option presents NO security for the visitor's wireless network, but it also requires no setup on the user's devices. All of the other options would require some sort of pre-shared key and setup to allow the visitor to use the network.

QUESTION 55:

You are working as part of a network installation team. Your team has been asked to install Cat 5e cabling to some new offices on the second floor of the building. Currently, the office only has one network closet which is located on the first floor. Your team spent the morning running 48 new CAT 5e cables from a patch panel in the networking closet on the first floor to a new networking closet you are outfitting on the second floor. Your team terminated these cables in a new patch panel in the 2nd floor closet. You measured the distance from the switch in the 1st floor closet to the new second floor patch panel and determined it was 80 meters. The team then ran cables from this patch panel to each of the new offices. Some of the offices are working properly, but others are not. You suspect that some of the cable runs are exceeding the maximum length allowed by Cat 5e cabling. What is the BEST solution to this problem?

1. Install a repeater between the patch panel and each office
2. Install a small switch in each office to increase the signal
3. Install a switch in the second floor networking closet to increase the signal
4. Install a hub in the second floor networking closet to increase the signal

Correct Answer(s): 3

Explanation:

The best option is to install a switch in the networking closet on the second floor which can connect to the cables coming from the first floor closet and then to the cables on the second floor patch panel. This will act as a repeater to boost the signal strength over the Cat5e cable, effectively resetting the cable length to 0 meters before leaving the closet. While a repeater may be a good option, a switch is more effective in this case since there are so many cables and repeaters usually only work for an individual cable. A hub would similarly work, but would introduce a signal collision domain for 48 computers. This would drastically decrease the performance of the network. Finally, we don't want to include a switch in each office, as this is a bad security practice and an inefficient use of resources. It is easier to manage and administer a single, centralized switch in the network closet.

QUESTION 56:

A technician is installing a network firewall and would like to block all WAN to LAN traffic that is using ports other than the default ports for Internet and email connectivity. What rule should the technician verify FIRST?

1. An implicit deny is enabled

2. All inbound traffic is blocked
3. A DMZ has been created
4. All outbound traffic is blocked

Correct Answer(s): 1

Explanation:

Implicit deny only allows certain traffic through that is specified by certain ports.

QUESTION 57:

You have been dispatched to investigate some sporadic network outages. After looking at the event logs for the network equipment, you found that the network equipment has been restarting at the same time every day. What should you implement to correct this issue?

1. Surge protector
2. UPS
3. Air flow management
4. Grounding bar

Correct Answer(s): 2

Explanation:

An Uninterruptible power supply (UPS) is a battery system that can supply short term power to electrical units. Since all the devices are restarting at the same time, it is likely due to a power outage. In this case, a UPS would continue to supply power to the network equipment during outages or blackouts.

QUESTION 58:

A network technician is asked to redesign an Ethernet network before some new monitoring software is added to each workstation on the network. The new software will broadcast statistics from each host to a monitoring server for each of the five departments in the company. The added network traffic is a concern of management that must be addressed. How should the technician design the new network?

1. Increase the number of switches on the network to reduce broadcasts
2. Increase the collision domains to compensate for the added broadcasts
3. Add a router and create a segment for all the monitoring host stations
4. Place each department in a separate VLAN

Correct Answer(s): 4

Explanation:

Placing each of the departments on separate VLANs will help minimize the added network traffic. VLANs work by taking multiple physical hosts and LANs and configuring them to act as if they were attached to the same Ethernet switch.

QUESTION 59:

Your supervisor has asked you to run a Cat 5e cable between two network switches in the server room. Which type of connector should be used with a Cat 5e cable?

1. DB-25
2. RS-232
3. RJ-45
4. RJ-11

Correct Answer(s): 3

Explanation:

A Cat 5e cable should uses a RJ-45 connector on each end of the cable. This is the standard type of connector for Cat 3, Cat 5, Cat 5e, and Cat 6a cables.

QUESTION 60:

A small real estate office has about 15 workstations and would like to use DHCP to assign classful IP addresses to each workstation. The subnet only has one octet for the host portion of each device. Which of the following IP addresses could be assigned as the default gateway?

1. 192.168.0.1
2. 172.16.0.1
3. 10.0.0.1
4. 169.254.0.1

Correct Answer(s): 1

Explanation:

A non-routable IP address (in this case 192.168.0.1), also known as a private IP address, is not assigned to any one organization and does not need to be assigned by an Internet Service Provider. Since the question wants a classful IP addressing scheme to be assigned to devices, and only one octet being available for the host portion, it would need to be a Class C address. The only Class C address to choose is

192.168.0.1 based on the options provided. The IP 10.0.0.1 is a Class A address. The IP 172.16.0.1 is a Class B address. The IP 169.254.0.01 is an APIPA (reserved) address.

QUESTION 61:

A home user reports that a speed test website shows the following information: Download speed: 33.3Mbps

Upload speed: 10.2Mbps Which of the following is the best interpretation of the results?

1. The home PC is receiving data at 33.3 Mbps and sending data at 10.2 Mbps.
2. The home PC downloaded 33.3 MB of data to the website and uploaded 10.2 MB of data to the website.
3. The website upload bandwidth is saturated and it does not match the download speed.
4. The website is downloading data to its server at 33.3 Mbps and uploading data from its server at 10.2 Mbps.

Correct Answer(s): 1

Explanation:

This connection is an asymmetric connection, like a cable modem or DSL, where upload and download speeds do not match.

QUESTION 62:

You are conducting a port scan of an older server on your network to determine what services are being run on it. You find that port 80 and 443 are open, but port 20 and 21 are reported as closed. All other ports are reported as FILTERED. Based on this report, what can you determine about the server?

1. The server is running as a web server and is denying any other service requests
2. The service is running a FTP server and it is denying any other service requests
3. The server is offline and not responding
4. The server is behind a firewall and is blocked from receiving any traffic

Correct Answer(s): 1

Explanation:

When a port scanner returns a result of CLOSED, it means the service is denying the inbound traffic on that port. In this case, it is denying FTP traffic on ports 20 and 21. This server is running a web server (port 80 and 443), but those are showing as OPEN and receiving traffic. All the FILTERED ports are being blocked by the network firewall.

QUESTION 63:

Users connecting to an SSID appear to be unable to authenticate to the captive portal. Which of the following is the MOST likely cause of the issue?

1. CSMA/CA
2. WPA2 security key
3. SSL certificates
4. RADIUS

Correct Answer(s): 4

Explanation:

Captive portals usually rely on 802.1x, and 802.1x uses RADIUS for authentication.

QUESTION 64:

Over the past week, the users of your network have reported that the network has been operating slowly. You have made some changes to the network to attempt to increase its speed and responsiveness, but your supervisor is requesting that you provide some proof that the network is actually faster and doesn't just "feel" faster. Which of the following should you use to prove that the current configuration has improved the speed of the network?

1. Present him with a logical network diagram showing the configuration changes
2. Provide him a copy of the approved change request for your configuration changes
3. Present him with a physical network diagram that shows the changes you made
4. Show him the results of a new performance baseline assessment

Correct Answer(s): 4

Explanation:

The only way to prove to your supervisor that the network is actually faster and more responsive is to conduct a new performance baseline and compare it to the results of the baseline that was created prior to the changes. By comparing the "current" speed against the "previous" baseline's speed, you can definitely prove if the network is indeed faster as a result of your configuration changes.

QUESTION 65:

Which of the following must be added to a VLAN with a gateway in order to add security to it?

1. A RADIUS server
2. 802.1d
3. 802.1w
4. An ACL

Correct Answer(s): 4

Explanation:

VLANs can be protected with an ACL. Without a properly configured ACL, there is no additional security provided by a VLAN.

QUESTION 66:

What is BEST used to perform a one-time temporary posture assessment in a NAC environment?

1. Antivirus
2. Host-based firewall
3. Non-persistent agent
4. Intrusion prevention system

Correct Answer(s): 3

Explanation:

A non-persistent agent is used to access the device during one-time check-in at login. This is beneficial in BYOD (Bring Your Own Device) policies.

QUESTION 67:

A technician is setting up a new network and wants to create redundant paths through the network. Which of the following should be implemented to prevent performance degradation within the network?

1. Port mirroring
2. ARP inspection
3. VLAN
4. Spanning tree

Correct Answer(s): 4

Explanation:

The Spanning Tree Protocol (STP) is a network protocol that builds a logical loop-free topology for Ethernet networks. The basic function of STP is to prevent bridge loops and the broadcast radiation that results from them. If you have redundant links setup, it is important to utilize STP to prevent loops within the network.

QUESTION 68:

You have configured your network into multiple segments by creating multiple broadcast domains. Which of the following devices should you use to allow the different network segments to communicate with each other?

1. Hub
2. Switch
3. Bridge
4. Router

Correct Answer(s): 4

Explanation:

A router is used to allow different network segments and broadcast domains to communicate with each other. If you have a Layer 3 switch, this will also function as a router and allow communication to occur. Since the question didn't specify if the switch was a layer 2 or layer 3 switch, we must assume it is a traditional layer 2 switch which cannot route traffic from one broadcast domain to the other broadcast domains.

QUESTION 69:

A company-wide audit revealed employees are using company laptops and desktops for personal use. To prevent this from occurring, in which document should the company incorporate the phrase "Company-owned IT assets are to be used to perform authorized company business only"?

1. AUP
2. SLA
3. MSA
4. MOU

Correct Answer(s): 1

Explanation:

Acceptable Use Policy dictates what types of actions an employee can or cannot do with company-issued IT equipment.

QUESTION 70:

You are working as a network technician and need to create several Cat 5e network cables to run between different computers and the network jacks on the wall. The connections between the switch and the patch panel, and the patch panel and the wall jacks have already been installed and tested. Which of the following tools would NOT be necessary to complete this task?

1. RJ-45 connectors
2. Wire stripper
3. Cable crimper
4. Punchdown tool

Correct Answer(s): 4

Explanation:

A punchdown tool is used to connect a network cable (such as Cat 5e) to a patch panel, 110-block, or the inside portion of a wall jack, therefore it is not needed for this task. A wire stripper is used to remove the outer plastic shielding from the Cat 5e cable so that you can reach the inner wiring pairs. The RJ-45 connectors are used to make the connection between the cable and a network jack, and the cable crimper is used to ensure the RJ-45 connector stays attached to the end of the Cat 5e cable.

QUESTION 71:

You are about to perform a major configuration upgrade to a network device. What should you have prepared in case the upgrade fails?

1. Business continuity plan
2. Vulnerability report

3. Rollback plan
4. Baseline report

Correct Answer(s): 3

Explanation:

The purpose of a rollback plan is to document at every point during the deployment of a change or upgrade where you can stop the deployment and return to a known-good state.

QUESTION 72:

You are assisting the company with developing a new business continuity plan. What would be the BEST recommendation to add to the BCP?

1. Perform recurring vulnerability scans
2. Build redundant links between core devices
3. Physically secure all network equipment
4. Maintain up-to-date configuration backups

Correct Answer(s): 2

Explanation:

The business continuity plan focuses on the tasks carried out by an organization to ensure that critical business functions continue to operate during and after a disaster. By keeping redundant links between core devices, critical business services can be kept running if one link is unavailable during a disaster. Some of the other options are good ideas, too, but this is the BEST choice.

QUESTION 73:

Exploiting a weakness in a user's wireless headset to compromise the mobile device is known as what?

1. Multiplexing
2. Zero-day attack
3. Smurfing
4. Bluejacking

Correct Answer(s): 4

Explanation:

Bluejacking is the sending of unsolicited messages over Bluetooth to Bluetooth-enabled devices such as mobile phones, PDAs, or laptop computers or sending a vCard which typically contains a message in the name field (i.e., for bluedating or bluechat) to another.

QUESTION 74:

Which of the following network topologies requires that all nodes have a point-to-point connection with each and every other node in the network?

1. Bus
2. Star
3. Mesh
4. Ring

Correct Answer(s): 3

Explanation:

A mesh network is a network topology in which each node relays data for the network. Because of this, physical mesh networks are very expensive to implement and not often used.

QUESTION 75:

What is used to authenticate remote workers who connect from offsite?

1. OSPF
2. VTP trunking
3. 802.1x
4. Virtual PBX

Correct Answer(s): 3

Explanation:

802.1x can be used because it is designed to enhance the security of wireless local area networks (WLANs) . WLANs provide an authentication framework, allowing a user to be authenticated by a central authority. RADIUS (Remote Authentication Dial-In User Service) allows a company to maintain user profiles in a central database that all remote servers can share. It provides better security, allowing a company to set up a policy that can be applied at a single administered network point. Remote users connect to one or more Remote Access Servers. The remote access servers then forward the authentication requests to the central RADIUS server. 802.1X is an IEEE Standard for Port-based Network Access Control (PNAC). It provides an authentication mechanism to devices wishing to attach to a network. 802.1X authentication involves three parties: a supplicant, an authenticator, and an authentication server. The supplicant is a client that wishes to attach to the network. The authenticator is a network device, such as an Ethernet switch, wireless access point or in this case, a remote access server and the authentication server is the RADIUS server.

Practice Exam #5

QUESTION 1:

(This is a simulated Performance-Based Question. On the real certification exam, you will be asked to click on the appropriate device to see and modify its configuration.)

Wireless network users recently began experiencing speed and performance issues on your network after Access Point 2 (AP2) was replaced due to a recent hardware failure. The original wireless network was installed according to a wireless consultant's specifications and has always worked properly without any issues in the past.

You have been asked to evaluate the situation and resolve any issues you find in order to improve both the performance and connectivity of the network. The client has instructed you to adjust the least amount of settings/configurations possible while you attempt to fix the issue. Before arriving on site, you have been giving the following floor plan of the office with a very basic network diagram drawn on top of it.

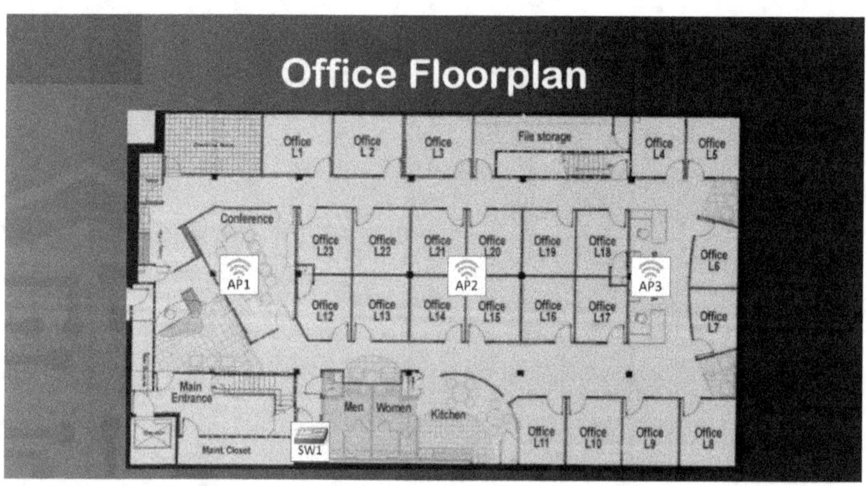

Based on the information provided to your so far, which network device would you log into first to begin your troubleshooting efforts?

1. AP1
2. AP2
3. AP3

4. SW1

Correct Answer(s): 2

Explanation:

Since everything was working properly on the network prior to AP2 being replaced after the recent hardware failure, it is likely that AP2 has some kind of configuration error that has led to the recent connectivity and performance problems. Therefore, you should begin your troubleshooting efforts with AP2.

QUESTION 2:

(This is a simulated Performance-Based Question. On the real certification exam, you would have to click on each device on the network diagram to open it and view/edit its configuration.)

Wireless network users recently began experiencing speed and performance issues on your network after Access Point 2 (AP2) was replaced due to a recent hardware failure. The original wireless network was installed according to a wireless consultant's specifications and has always worked properly without any issues in the past. Now that you are at the client's office, you logged into each of the devices and see the following configuration settings.

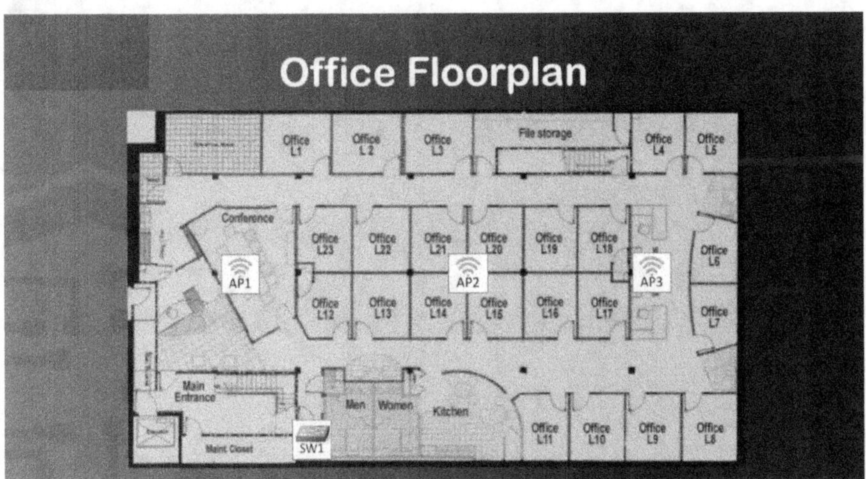

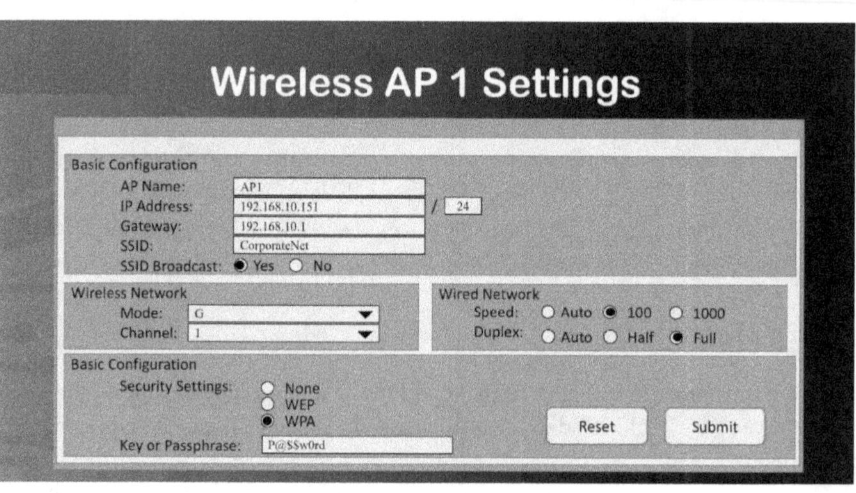

Wireless AP 1 Settings
Basic Configuration
AP Name: AP1
IP Address: 192.168.10.151 / 24
Gateway: 192.168.10.1
SSID: CorporateNet
SSID Broadcast: Yes No
Wireless Network
Mode: G
Channel: 1
Wired Network
Speed: Auto 100 1000
Duplex: Auto Half Full
Basic Configuration
Security Settings: None WEP WPA
Reset Submit
Key or Passphrase: P@$$w0rd

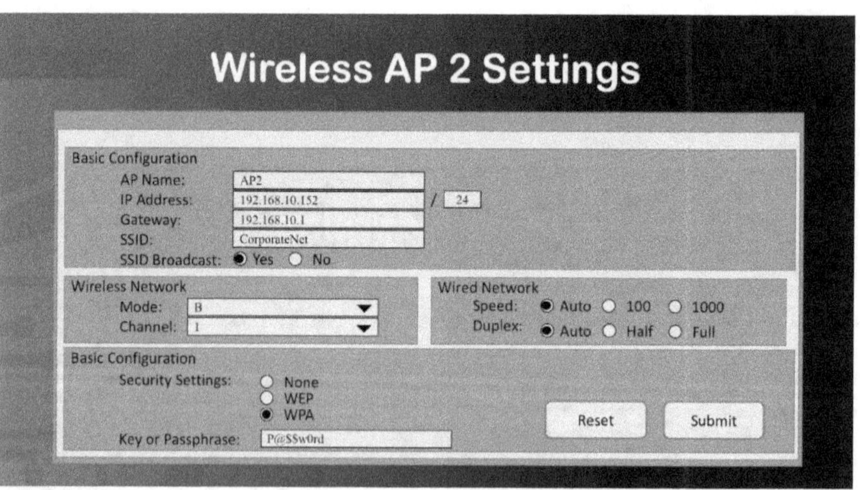

Wireless AP 2 Settings
Basic Configuration
AP Name: AP2
IP Address: 192.168.10.152 / 24
Gateway: 192.168.10.1
SSID: CorporateNet
SSID Broadcast: Yes No
Wireless Network
Mode: B
Channel: 1
Wired Network
Speed: Auto 100 1000
Duplex: Auto Half Full
Basic Configuration
Security Settings: None WEP WPA
Reset Submit
Key or Passphrase: P@$$w0rd

Wireless AP 3 Settings

Basic Configuration
AP Name: AP3
IP Address: 192.168.10.153 / 24
Gateway: 192.168.10.1
SSID: CorporateNet
SSID Broadcast: ● Yes ○ No

Wireless Network
Mode: G
Channel: 11

Wired Network
Speed: ○ Auto ● 100 ○ 1000
Duplex: ○ Auto ○ Half ● Full

Basic Configuration
Security Settings: ○ None ○ WEP ● WPA
Key or Passphrase: P@SSw0rd

Reset   Submit

Based on the configurations shown, which of the following should you change to bring the wireless network back to optimal performance? (Please select any or all options that apply)

1. Change AP2's Channel from 1 to 6
2. Change AP1's Channel from 1 to 6
3. Change AP2's Mode from B to G
4. Change AP1's and AP3's Mode from G to B
5. Change AP2 from Auto/Auto to 100/Full

Correct Answer(s): 1, 3, 5

Explanation:

By comparing the configurations on the three different APs, we can see that AP1 and AP3 are set on channels 1 and 11, but AP2 is set to channel 1. This will cause interference. Therefore, you should change AP2 to channel 6 to avoid interference. Also, AP1 and AP3 are using Wireless G (which support 54 mbps), but AP2 is set to Wireless B (only 11 mbps). This is causing the performance issue, so AP2 should be set to Wireless G to match the rest of the network. Finally, AP2 is set to Auto/Auto, but AP1 and AP3 are set to 100/Full. For best performance, AP2 should be set to 100/Full to match AP1 and AP3.

QUESTION 3:

(This is a simulated Performance-Based Question.)

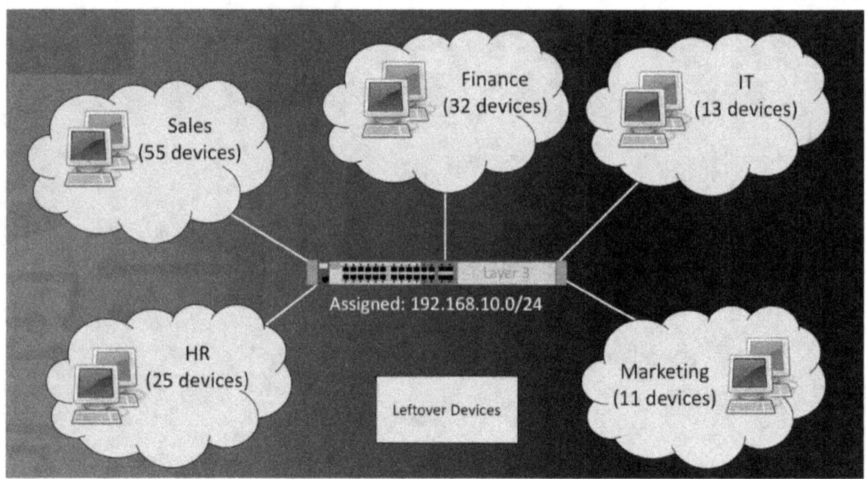

The company's corporate headquarters provided your branch office a portion of their Class C subnet to use at a new office location. You must allocate the minimum number of addresses using CIDR notation in order to accommodate each department's needs. What is the correct CIDR notation for the Human Resources (HR) department's subnet which requires 25 devices?

1. /25
2. /26
3. /27
4. /28
5. /29
6. /30

Correct Answer(s): 3

Explanation:

Since the HR department needs 25 devices plus a network ID and broadcast IP, it will require 27 IP addresses. The smallest subnet that can fit 27 IPs is a /27 (32 IPs).

QUESTION 4:

(This is a simulated Performance-Based Question.) What ports do HTTPS and RDP utilize?

1. 443, 25
2. 443, 161

3. 443, 3389
4. 443, 445

Correct Answer(s): 3

Explanation:

HTTPS (Hyper Text Transfer Protocol Secure) uses port 443. RDP (Remote Desktop Protocol) uses port 3389. If this was a question on the real exam, you would see a list of ports on one side and a list of protocols on the other, and you would drag and drop each one to match them up.

QUESTION 5:

(This is a simulated Performance-Based Question.)

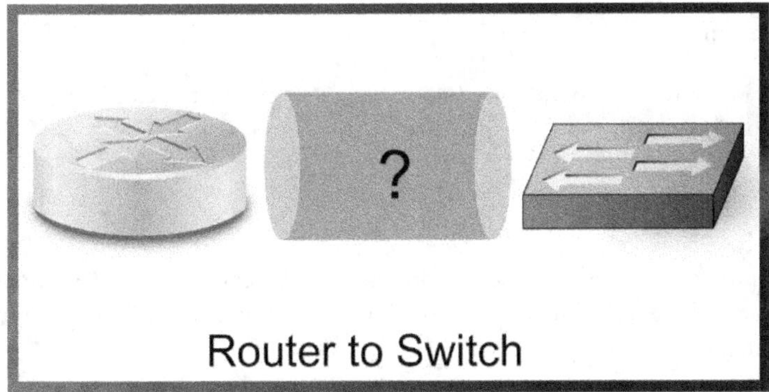

What type of cable would you use to connect a router to a switch?

1. Crossover
2. RG-6
3. Rollover
4. RS-232
5. Straight-through

Correct Answer(s): 5

Explanation:

When connecting switches to routers, you can just use a straight-through cable because switches are DCE and routers are DTE devices. When you connect a (switch/hub) to a (switch/hub), you need a crossover. If you connect a (switch/hub) to a (router/computer), you need a straight through. If you connect a (router/computer) to (router/computer), then you need a crossover. If this was a real question on the exam, you would have the words provided in a list, and you would drag them below the appropriate drawing.

QUESTION 6:

During what period should all scheduled work on production network equipment be conducted?

1. Maintenance window
2. Development life cycle
3. Down time
4. Business hours

Correct Answer(s): 1

Explanation:

By using a Maintenance Window, all downtime is limited and the organization can prepare in advance for the scheduled work to be carried out.

QUESTION 7:

You want to ensure that only one person can enter or leave the server room at a time. Which of the following physical security devices would BEST help you meet this requirement?

1. Cipher lock
2. Thumbprint reader
3. Video monitoring
4. Mantrap

Correct Answer(s): 4

Explanation:

A mantrap allows you to enter one door and wait for it to close before entering another door. Video monitoring is a passive security feature, so it won't prevent two people from entering at once. The thumbprint reader or cipher lock will ensure that only an authorized user can open the door, but it won't prevent someone from piggybacking and entering with them.

QUESTION 8:

The network technician has received a large number of complaints from users that there is poor network performance. The network technician suspects a user may have created a malicious flood on the network with a large number of ping requests. What should the technician do?

1. Block all ICMP request
2. Update all antivirus software
3. Remove all suspected users from the network
4. Upgrade firmware on all network cards

Correct Answer(s): 1

Explanation:

Ping requests use the Internet Control Message Protocol to send operational information about a host or router. Blocking all ICMP requests would eliminate the ping request flood, although it may become harder to diagnose network issues in the future as ICMP is used heavily in network troubleshooting.

QUESTION 9:

A network technician is responsible for the basic security of the network. Management has asked if there is a way to improve the level of access users have to the company file server. Right now, any employee can upload and download files with basic system authentication (username and password). What should he configure to increase security?

1. Kerberos authentication
2. MDS authentication
3. Multi-factor authentication
4. Single sign-on authentication

Correct Answer(s): 3

Explanation:

This security approach provides a defense layer that makes it difficult for an unauthorized user to break into a system. It provides multiple factors that a user must know in order to obtain access. For instance, if one factor is successfully broken, there will be few others that the individual attempting to enter the system must overcome.

QUESTION 10:

John is investigating a performance issue on a server and has begun by gathering the server's utilization statistics. John notices that the statistics are outside of the normal acceptable ranges. What should John do next?

1. Archive the logs
2. Conduct a vulnerability scan
3. Conduct a baseline review
4. Conduct a port scan

Correct Answer(s): 3

Explanation:

John should conduct a baseline review to compare the statistics he collected against the previous baseline. He can then use this information to further investigate the cause of the drop in the server's performance.

QUESTION 11:

After a recent breach, the security technician decides the company needs to analyze and aggregate its security logs. Which system should be used?

1. Event log
2. Syslog
3. SIEM
4. SNMP

Correct Answer(s): 3

Explanation:

Using a Security information and event management (SIEM) product, the security logs can be analyzed and aggregated. SIEM is a term for software products and services combining security information management (SIM) and security event management (SEM).

QUESTION 12:

Your company has installed a guest wireless network in the break room. According to company policy, employees may only connect to the network and use it while on their lunch break. Which of the following policies should you have each employee sign to show they understand and accept the conditions of use for this guest network?

1. MOU
2. AUP
3. SLA
4. NDA

Correct Answer(s): 2

Explanation:

An acceptable use policy (AUP), acceptable usage policy or fair use policy, is a set of rules applied by the owner, creator or administrator of a network, website, or service, that restrict the ways in which the network, website or system may be used and sets guidelines as to how it should be used. In this scenario, this is the most appropriate policy to utilize.

QUESTION 13:

You need to connect to a Linux server to conduct some maintenance. The server is located in a remote office about 50 miles from your own. You decide to connect the server remotely instead of driving to the location to save some time, but you want to ensure you do this securely. The Linux server has VNC installed, but it isn't configured to provide an encrypted connection. Which of the following should you use to secure the VNC connection to the remote server?

1. HTTPS
2. SSH in tunnel mode
3. RDP
4. WPA2

Correct Answer(s): 2

Explanation:

Since you want to use the existing VNC server to make the connection and it is unencrypted, you should tunnel the VNC protocol through a secure SSH connection to encrypt it. While an SSH client connects to a Secure Shell server, which allows you to run terminal commands as if you were sitting in front of another computer, it can also allow you to "tunnel" any port or protocol between your local system and a remote SSH server through its own encryption process. This allows you to add a layer of encryption and security to an unsecured protocol or application.

QUESTION 14:

A project lead is reviewing the statement of work for an upcoming project that is focused on identifying potential weaknesses in the organization's internal and external network infrastructure. As part of the project, a team of external contractors will attempt to employ various attacks against the organization. The statement of work specifically addresses the utilization of an automated tool to probe network resources in an attempt to develop logical diagrams indicating weaknesses in the infrastructure. The scope of activity as described in the statement of work is an example of:

1. Session hijacking
2. Vulnerability scanning
3. Social engineering
4. Penetration testing

Correct Answer(s): 4

Explanation:

Penetration testing is the act of using a computer system, an individual network, or another application to find vulnerabilities that an attacker could use to compromise your systems. Penetration testing can also find endpoints with vulnerabilities which makes the attack surface greater.

QUESTION 15:

You just arrived at school today, pulled your laptop out of your backpack, and tried to connect your laptop to the Wi-Fi network. It worked fine yesterday, but today it won't connect automatically or display any available networks. You haven't done anything to the laptop since you left class yesterday. You ask your classmates if they are able to connect to the Wifi and every one of them is connected without any issues. What should you check FIRST in your attempt to connect your laptop to the Wifi?

1. Wireless controller configuration
2. IP address issued by the DHCP server
3. Wireless switch on your laptop
4. The configuration of the WAP

Correct Answer(s): 3

Explanation:

Since everyone else's laptops are connected without any issues, the problem is not with the network but with your laptop in some form. This rules out the wireless controller configuration or WAP settings since those are both things that would affect all users on the network. Since you are not connected or finding any networks, you won't have a DHCP address assigned. The most likely cause of your issue is that the wireless switch on your laptop was accidentally switched to the off position when you put your laptop in your backpack. (Note: Not all laptops have a wireless switch, but from the options provided, this is the most logical answer. If you have a MacBook, for example, they do not use a physical wireless switch.)

QUESTION 16:

Dion Training is considering moving its headquarters and data center to Florida, but they are worried about hurricanes disrupting their business operations. To mitigate this risk, Dion Training has signed a contract with a vendor located in a different state to provide hardware, software, and the procedures necessary for the company to recover quickly in the case of a catastrophic event, like a hurricane causing a power loss for up to 10 days. Jason, as the owner, is a little concerned that this contract isn't sufficient to mitigate enough of the risk since it only provides a solution for the first 10 days. Jason wonders, "what will we do if a major outage occurs and our offices are not able to be used for 6-12 months?" Jason has hired you on to help develop Dion Training's long-term strategy for recovering from such an event. What type of plan should you create?

1. Incident response plan
2. Disaster recovery plan
3. Business continuity plan
4. Risk management plan

Correct Answer(s): 3

Explanation:

A business continuity plan (BCP) is a plan to help ensure that business processes can continue during a time of emergency or disaster. Such emergencies or disasters might include a fire or any other case where business is not able to occur under normal conditions. A disaster recovery plan is useful (and usually a piece of the large business continuity plan), but it is insufficient for the long-term strategy which is needed to support business operations during an extended outage.

QUESTION 17:

A technician is attempting to resolve an issue with users on the network not being able to access websites. The technician pings the default gateway and DNS servers successfully. Pinging a website by URL is unsuccessful but using a known IP address is successful. What would resolve the issue?

1. Update the HOST file with the URLs for all websites
2. Use NSLOOKUP to resolve URLs
3. Ensure ICMP messages can pass through the firewall
4. Enable port 53 on the firewall

Correct Answer(s): 4

Explanation:

Port 53 is used by DNS. The DNS Server is used to translate FQDN to IP addresses.

QUESTION 18:

A network technician responds to a customer reporting that a workstation continually loses the connection to the network. The user explains that it occurs randomly and it happens several times throughout the day. Which step of the troubleshooting method should the technician perform first?

1.   Test the theory
2.   Establish a plan of action
3.   Gather information
4.   Question the obvious

Correct Answer(s): 3

Explanation:

In order to have a good understanding and a clear idea on what the issue could be, the technician should gather information as the first step.

QUESTION 19:

The Chief Security Officer is concerned with the possible theft of corporate data from the network. He wants to ensure that any sensitive data cannot be exfiltrated from the network. Which of the following should be implemented to BEST mitigate this threat?

1.   AUP
2.   DLP
3.   NDA
4.   MOU

Correct Answer(s): 2

Explanation:

Data loss prevention (DLP) systems are used to ensure that end users do not send sensitive or critical information outside the corporate network. These DLP products help a network administrator control what data end users can transfer. While an Acceptable Use Policy (AUP), Non Disclosure Agreement (NDA), or MOU (Memorandum of Understanding) might provide some administrative controls to help mitigate the threat of data loss or theft, a DLP is the BEST solution as it provides a technical way to enforce your policies.

QUESTION 20:

A network administrator recently set up a network computer lab and discovered some connectivity issues. The administrator is able to ping the fiber uplink interface, but none of the new PCs plugged into the switch respond to ICMP requests. What should the technician do next?

1. Check if there are link lights on the ports
2. Check the ports on the switch for full duplex
3. Check to see if port security is enabled
4. Check to see if the uplink interface is configured correctly

Correct Answer(s): 1

Explanation:

By checking the link lights on the ports, the administrator can verify if there is any activity on the network, if the ports are enabled, and if the Layer 1 components are working correctly.

QUESTION 21:

Which of the following cloud infrastructures includes on-premise servers utilizing a centralized syslog server that is hosted at a third-party organization in order to review the logs?

1. Hybrid
2. Public
3. Community
4. Private

Correct Answer(s): 1

Explanation:

On-premise servers is an aspect of the private cloud, whereas syslog hosted on a third-party server is an aspect of the public cloud. Since a hybrid cloud consists of any type of cloud computing sharing multiple aspects of different cloud infrastructure designs, hybrid is the correct answer.

QUESTION 22:

You have been asked to configure a router. Which of the following protocols should you enable to allow the router to determine the path to another network?

1. BGP
2. RTP
3. NTP
4. STP

Correct Answer(s): 1

Explanation:

BGP (Border Gateway Protocol) is a protocol that operates at layer 3 of the OSI model. Since the question asks about a router, you need to identify a routing protocol since this would enable the router to determine the path to another network using IP (layer 3) information. The other protocols listed are not routing protocols: RTP (Real-time Transport Protocol), NTP (Network Time Protocol), and STP (Spanning Tree Protocol).

QUESTION 23:

Which of the following ports should be allowed to provide access to certain VoIP applications?

1. 110
2. 139
3. 1720
4. 5060

Correct Answer(s): 4

Explanation:

5060 is used by SIP, which VOIP relies upon.

QUESTION 24:

IPv4 addresses are written using Base 10 numbers while IPv6 addresses are written in Base 16 numbers. What type of notation does Base16 utilize?

1. Octet
2. Binary
3. Hexadecimal
4. Decimal

Correct Answer(s): 3

Explanation:

Hexadecimal (or Hex for short) is the system of numbering that uses Base16. This includes the numbers 0, 1, 2, 3, 4, 5, 6, 7, 8, 9, A, B, C, D, E, and F.

QUESTION 25:

A switch technician is being tasked to centrally manage the switches and to segment the switches by broadcast domains. The corporate network is currently using VLAN 1 for all of its devices and is using a single private IP address range with a 24-bit mask. The supervisor wants VLAN 100 to be the management subnet and all switches to share the VLAN information. What option would be best to use?

1. Use VLSM on the IP address range, with STP and 802.1q on the inter switch connections with native VLAN 100
2. Use VLSM on the IP address range with VTP and 802.1x on all inter switch connections with native VLAN 100
3. Use VLSM on VLAN1, with VTP and 802.1w on the inter switch connections with native VLAN 100
4. Use VLSM on the IP address range with VTP and 802.1q on the inter switch connections with native VLAN 100

Correct Answer(s): 4

Explanation:

802.1q is the networking standard that supports VLANs and VLAN tagging. VTP is the VLAN Trunk Protocol and carries all VLAN information to all switches in a VTP domain.

QUESTION 26:

An administrator has a physical server with a single NIC. The administrator intends to deploy two virtual machines onto a single physical server. Each virtual machine needs two NICs, one that connects to the network, and a second that is a server to server heartbeat connection between the two virtual machines. After deploying the virtual machines, which of the following should the administrator do to meet the requirements?

1. The administrator should create a virtual switch for each guest; each switch should be configured for inter-switch links and the primary NIC should have a NAT to the corporate network

2. The administrator should create a virtual switch that is bridged to the corporate network, and a second virtual switch that carries intra-VM communication only
3. The administrator should create a virtual switch to bridge all of the connections to the network; the virtual heartbeat NICs should be set to addresses in an unused range
4. The administrator should install a second physical NIC onto the host, and then connect each guest machine's NICs to a dedicated physical NIC

Correct Answer(s): 3

Explanation:

By bridging all of the connections to the network, it allows for faster communication between the virtual machines (hosts). The heartbeat is set on unused address range in order to ensure there is no chance of data collision or loss of signal.

QUESTION 27:

A network engineer has been tasked with designing a network for a new branch office with approximately 50 network devices. This branch office will connect to the other offices via a MAN. Many of the other branch offices use off-the-shelf SOHO equipment. It is a requirement that the routing protocol chosen use the least amount of overhead. Additionally, all the computers on the network will be part of a single VLAN. The connection between these computers should produce the highest throughput possible in the most cost effective manner. What devices would be MOST appropriate?

1. A router should be used as a gateway device, with RIPv2 as the routing protocol. The computers should be connected to one another with a Gigabit Layer 2 switch.
2. A UTM should be used as a gateway device, with BGP as the routing protocol. The computers should be connected to one another using 1Gb Fibre Channel.
3. A router should be used as a gateway device, with EIGRP as the routing protocol. The computers should be connected to one another using a single 802.11N MIMO access point.
4. A router should be used as a gateway device, with OSPF as the routing protocol. The computers should be connected to one another using a Gigabit Layer 3 switch.

Correct Answer(s): 1

Explanation:

A Gigabit Layer 2 switch is the cheapest switching solution offering 1Gbps network connectivity between the computers. RIPv2 has a lower overhead as set forth in the requirements.

QUESTION 28:

A network administrator wants to increase the speed and fault tolerance of a connection between two network switches. To achieve this, which protocol should the administrator use?

1. LACP
2. LLDP
3. L2TP
4. LDAP

Correct Answer(s): 1

Explanation:

The Link Aggregation Control Protocol (LACP) provides a method to control the bundling of several physical ports together to form a single logical channel. The Link Layer Discovery Protocol (LLDP) is a vendor-neutral link layer protocol used by network devices for advertising their identity, capabilities, and neighbors on an IEEE 802 local area network, principally wired Ethernet. The Layer 2 Tunneling Protocol (L2TP) is a tunneling protocol used to support virtual private networks (VPNs) or as part of the delivery of services by ISPs. The Lightweight Directory Access Protocol (LDAP) is an open, vendor-neutral, industry standard application protocol for accessing and maintaining distributed directory information services over an Internet Protocol network.

QUESTION 29:

You are currently troubleshooting a network connection error. When you ping the default gateway, you receive no reply. You checked the default gateway and it is functioning properly, but the gateway cannot connect to any of the workstations on the network. At which layer of the OSI model do you believe the issue is occurring?

1. Presentation
2. Transport
3. Session
4. Physical

Correct Answer(s): 4

Explanation:

Ping requests occur at layer 3 (Network layer). Therefore, the problem could exist in layer 1 (physical), layer 2 (data link), or layer 3 (network). Since Physical (layer 1) is the only choice from layers 1-3 given, it must be the correct answer. Also, since the gateway cannot reach any of the other devices on the network, it is most likely a cable (physical) issue between the gateway and the network switch.

QUESTION 30:

You are working for a brand new startup company who recently moved into an old office building because the CEO liked the "charm" of the place. You have been tasked with converting a small janitorial closet into an IDF to support the new office network. You measure the closet and determine that you can install a two-post rack inside of it, and all your necessary networking equipment will fit in the two-post rack. You test the power outlet that was installed in the closet, and it is sufficient for your needs. What is the NEXT thing you should be concerned with to ensure this closet can be used as your IDF?

1. Is there redundant power available?
2. Can I install a UPS in this closet?
3. Is there adequate air flow and cooling in the closet?
4. How will I label the cables during installation?

Correct Answer(s): 3

Explanation:

Since you are converting an old closet into an IDF, you need to ensure you have 3 main things first: Power, Space, and Cooling. You already verified there was adequate power and space, so now you need to determine if there is adequate air flow and cooling to prevent the equipment from overheating. After that, you can then move into determining how to supply backup power (UPS or redundancy).

QUESTION 31:

You have been asked to create an allow statement on the firewall's ACL to allow NTP traffic to pass into the network. Which port should be included?

1. 69
2. 123
3. 143
4. 636

Correct Answer(s): 2

Explanation:

The correct port for NTP is 123. Port 69 is used for TFTP. Port 143 is used for IMAP. Port 636 is used for LDAPS.

QUESTION 32:

The administrator modifies a rule on the firewall and now all the FTP users cannot access the server any longer. The manager calls the administrator and asks what caused the extreme downtime for the server. In regards to the manager's inquiry, what did the administrator forget to do first?

1. Submit a change request
2. Schedule a maintenance window
3. Provide notification of change to users
4. Document the changes

Correct Answer(s): 1

Explanation:

A change request should be submitted through the change management process prior to any changes being made.

QUESTION 33:

You have just replaced a faulty Ethernet cable in a patch panel. Within a few minutes, you find out that users are experiencing slow or no Internet connectivity all over the building. A broadcast storm has begun to occur. After removing the replacement cable, which of the following should you do NEXT?

1. Replace the cable during the next maintenance window
2. Review labeling and logical network diagram documentation
3. Attempt to isolate the storm to the domain by rebooting the switch
4. Remove and replace all of the other Ethernet cables on the switch to isolate the issue

Correct Answer(s): 2

Explanation:

You most likely have plugged the new cable into the wrong port on the patch panel. By reviewing the documentation and labeling, you might be able to see the domain architecture, the strength of user connections, and the relationships in those connections, thereby making it easy to reassign the patch cables corrected. It is likely that something has been mislabeled, and the replacement of the patch cable was plugged into the wrong port and caused a loop.

QUESTION 34:

A network administrator wants to logically separate web servers on the network. Which of the following network device will need to be configured?

1. IPS
2. Switch
3. Hub
4. HIDS

Correct Answer(s): 2

Explanation:

Logical separation of network devices is accomplished using VLANs, which is configured on the network switches.

QUESTION 35:

Your local city council is trying to revitalize the old downtown area. One council member believes that if they provided free wireless coverage throughout the entire old downtown area that it will attract more Generation Y and Millennials to the area because they love being constantly connected to the internet. Which type of network geography BEST describes this proposed large scale wireless network?

1. WAN
2. MAN
3. LAN
4. PAN

Correct Answer(s): 2

Explanation:

A metropolitan area network (MAN) is a computer network that interconnects users with computer resources in a geographic area or region larger than that covered by even a large local area network (LAN) but smaller than the area covered by a wide area network (WAN). A MAN usually covers several blocks of a city or metropolitan area, but could be expanded to cover the entire city, as well.

QUESTION 36:

A user is receiving certificate errors in other languages within their web browser when they try to access your company's website. Which of the following is the MOST likely cause of this issue?

1. DoS
2. Reflective DNS
3. Man-in-the-middle
4. ARP poisoning

Correct Answer(s): 3

Explanation:

A man-in-the-middle attack is a general term for when a perpetrator positions himself in a conversation between a user and an application, either to eavesdrop or to impersonate one of the parties, making it appear as if a normal exchange of information is occurring. For example, if your user and server are both in the United States (English language), but the attacker performing the MITM is from Russia, then the user may see a certificate error in Russian instead of English.

QUESTION 37:

Your company has been asked by a local charity that supports underprivileged youth if they would help to build an internet café for their students. Because the charity doesn't have any funding for this project, your company has decided to donate their old workstations and networking equipment to create the network. All of the workstations, routers, and switches have been tested prior to installation. To save money, the company has decided to reuse some old network cable to connect the computers to the switches. When you arrive at the new internet cafe, you are told that everything is working except unlucky computer #13 can't connect to the network. You attempt to plug the network cable into another computer, but then that computer also cannot connect to the network. Confused, you try connecting the cable directly between two computers, and now they can communicate directly between each other. What is wrong with this cable?

1. The cable is a Cat 3 cable and should be replaced with a CAT 5e cable
2. The cable is a rollover cable
3. The cable is a crossover cable but should be a straight through cable
4. The cable is a straight through cable but should be a crossover cable

Correct Answer(s): 3

Explanation:

Since the cable only worked when connecting two computers directly together, it is a crossover cable. Crossover cables are used to connect two of the same types of devices (computer to computer, or router to router) by switching the transmit and receive pins in the cable's jack. Since you are trying to connect a computer to a switch, you need to have a straight-through cable instead.

QUESTION 38:

The administrator would like to use the strongest encryption level possible using PSK without utilizing an additional authentication server. What encryption type should be implemented?

1. WPA2 Enterprise
2. WEP
3. MAC filtering
4. WPA personal

Correct Answer(s): 4

Explanation:

Since he wishes to use a pre-shared key and not require an authentication server, the most secure choice is WPA personal. If WPA2 Personal was an option, it would be more secure, though. The reason WPA2 Enterprise is incorrect is because the requirement was for a PSK, whereas WPA2 Enterprise requires a RADIUS authentication server to be used.

QUESTION 39:

A network technician has received a report that workstations are unable to gain access to the network. During the troubleshooting process, the technician discovers that the switch connecting these workstations has failed. Which of the following is the QUICKEST option to configure a replacement switch?

1. Baseline
2. Image
3. Archive
4. Syslog

Correct Answer(s): 2

Explanation:

The baseline is only to give you an idea on how it works before any changes are made. The archive won't explain much and syslog is a windows feature. Process of elimination shows that an image would work best. To image a switch, you can make a backup of the configuration and deploy it to a new/different switch.

QUESTION 40:

You are trying to connect to another server on the network, but are unable to do so. You have determined that the other server is located on the 10.0.0.1/24 network but your workstation is located on the 192.168.1.1/24 network. Which of the following tools should you use to begin troubleshooting the connection between your workstation and the server?

1. ifconfig
2. traceroute
3. netstat
4. dig

Correct Answer(s): 2

Explanation:

Tracert is a command-line utility that is used to trace the path of an IP packet as it moves from its source to its destination. While using ping will tell you if the remote website is reachable or not, it will not tell you where the connection is broken. Tracert, though, performs a series of ICMP echo requests to determine which device in the connection path is not responding appropriately. This will help to identify if the connectivity issue lies within your workstation and the server since the traffic must be routed between the two networks.

QUESTION 41:

A network technician has designed a network consisting of an external Internet connection, a DMZ, an internal private network, and an administrative network. From which network segment should all routers and switches be configured to accept SSH connections?

1. Internal network since it is private
2. Administrative network allowing only admin access
3. DMZ only allowing access from the segment with the servers
4. Internet connection to allow admin access from anywhere

Correct Answer(s): 2

Explanation:

Since the admin network is hidden behind firewalls (surrounding the DMZ), SSH connections from the admin network are inherently secure and therefore should be allowed to communicate with the other three networks.

QUESTION 42:

A network technician has been asked to make the connections necessary to add video transported via fiber optics to the LAN within a building. There will be one fiber connector for the Tx port and another connector for the Rx port. Which of the following is the MOST common connector that will be used on the switch to connect the media converter?

1. FDDI
2. Fiber coupler
3. RJ-45
4. ST

Correct Answer(s): 4

Explanation:

Straight Tip (ST) fiber connections are the most common ones used in fiber optic connections in LAN networking applications, therefore this is most likely the correct answer.

QUESTION 43:

Which media type would employ the DOCSIS standard in a residential Internet installation?

1. Fiber
2. DSL
3. Cable
4. Cellular

Correct Answer(s): 3

Explanation:

Cable uses DOCSIS (Data over Cable Service Interface Specifications). This allows high-speed data transfer over an existing cable TV system.

QUESTION 44:

A network technician at a warehouse must implement a solution that will allow a company to track shipments as they enter and leave the facility. The warehouse workers must be able to scan and concurrently upload large images of items to a centralized server. Which of the following technologies should they utilize to meet these requirements?

1. 802.11ac
2. P2P
3. Bluetooth
4. IR

Correct Answer(s): 1

Explanation:

802.11ac is a very fast high-speed Wi-Fi network capable of 1 Gbps speeds over a 5 Ghz spectrum – perfect for uploading large image files quickly. Additionally, the warehouse might want to also utilize RFID to allow for the accurate scanning of items using radio frequency tracking tags.

QUESTION 45:

Mallory is very unhappy at her job at a large beverage company. She decides to steal sensitive information about the company's proprietary formula for a new energy drink. She installs a keylogger onto some of the product team's workstations, which then emails out the information to her personal email account each evening so she can post the information to WikiLeaks. How would you best classify Mallory and her actions?

1. Social engineering
2. Insider threat
3. Logic bomb
4. DoS

Correct Answer(s): 2

Explanation:

Mallory is considered an insider threat in this scenario. An insider threat is a malicious threat to an organization that comes from people within the organization, such as employees, former employees, contractors or business associates, who have inside information concerning the organization's security practices, data, and computer systems. Regardless of her method of stealing the information, the key to this question resides in the fact that she is an employee of the company doing something malicious.

QUESTION 46:

When two or more links are needed to pass network traffic as if they were one physical link, which of the following technologies should be used to satisfy the requirement?

1. 802.11af
2. 802.1w
3. LACP
4. VTP

Correct Answer(s): 3

Explanation:

The Link Aggregation Control Protocol (LACP) enables you to assign multiple physical links to a logical interface that will appear as a single link to a route processor.

QUESTION 47:

A network technician has downloaded the latest operating system of a particular vendor's switch. This update includes new features and enhancements. What should the technician perform FIRST when updating the switch's operating systems?

1. Backup the current configuration for each switch
2. Install during non-business hours to test the system
3. Test the O/S on one of the production switches
4. Power cycle the company's border router

Correct Answer(s): 1

Explanation:

A preventive method is always to backup the current configuration to the NVRAM (SW# copy run start) in case the newly-downloaded Operating System doesn't work properly. This would allow the technician to restore the switch from the previous backup.

QUESTION 48:

A company has had several virus infections over the past few months. The infections were caused by vulnerabilities in the application versions that are being used. What should an administrator implement to prevent future outbreaks?

1. Host-based intrusion detection systems
2. Acceptable use policies
3. Incident response team
4. Patch management

Correct Answer(s): 4

Explanation:

Since the viruses exploited known vulnerabilities, there should be patches available from the manufacturer/vendor. Based on this, proper patch management would prevent future outbreaks.

QUESTION 49:

A network technician must allow the use of HTTP traffic from the Internet over port 80 to an internal server running HTTP over port 81. Which of the following is this an example of?

1. Dynamic DNS
2. Virtual Private Networking (VPN)
3. Dynamic NAT
4. Port Forwarding

Correct Answer(s): 4

Explanation:

Port forwarding is an application of network address translation (NAT) that redirects a communication request from one address and port number combination to another while the packets are traversing a network gateway, such as a router or firewall.

QUESTION 50:

Dion Training wants to purchase an email marketing solution to better communicate with their students. A promising new startup has a new offering to provide access to their product from a central location rather than requiring Dion Training to internally host the product on their own network. Dion Training wants to ensure that their sensitive corporate information is not accessible by any of the startup's other clients.

Which type of cloud server should Dion Training look to purchase to meet these needs?

1. Public SaaS
2. Private SaaS
3. Hybrid IaaS
4. Community IaaS

Correct Answer(s): 2

Explanation:

SaaS (Software as a Service) is a cloud model whereby a service provider provides a software service and makes the service available to customers over the Internet. Examples of Saas include Microsoft Office 365, Microsoft Exchange Online, and Google Docs. Because of the concerns with sensitive corporate information being processed by the SaaS, Dion Training should ensure a Private SaaS is chosen. A private cloud is a particular model of cloud computing that involves a distinct and secure cloud based environment in which only the specified client (Dion Training in this case) can operate.

QUESTION 51:

A network engineer is designing a wireless network that uses multiple access points for complete coverage. Which of the following channel selections would result in the LEAST amount of interference between each access point?

1. Adjacent access point should be assigned channels 1, 6, and 11 with a 20MHz channel width.
2. Adjacent access points should be assigned channels 2, 6, and 10 with a 20MHz channel width.
3. Adjacent access points should be assigned channels 7 and 11 with a 40MHz channel width.
4. Adjacent access points should be assigned channels 8 and 11 with a 40MHz channel width

Correct Answer(s): 1

Explanation:

Because the overlapping signals are from access points that come from unrelated non-overlapping channels, the access points are least likely to interfere with each other. For Wireless B and G networks, you should always use channels 1, 6, and 11.

QUESTION 52:

You are installing a network for a new law firm in your area. They have stated that they must have a guaranteed throughput rate on their Internet connection. Based on this requirement, what type of WAN connection should you recommend?

1. Dial-up
2. Cable broadband
3. T-1
4. DSL

Correct Answer(s): 3

Explanation:

A T-1 connection provides a guaranteed 1.544 mbps of throughput. Dial-up, DSL, and cable broadband do not provide a guaranteed throughput rate. Instead, these services provide a variable throughput rate based on network conditions and demand in the area of your business.

QUESTION 53:

You run the command IPCONFIG on your laptop and see that you have been assigned an IP address of 169.254.0.1. Which category of IPv4 address is this?

1. APIPA
2. Private
3. Static
4. Public

Correct Answer(s): 1

Explanation:

APIPA stands for Automatic Private IP Addressing and is a feature of Windows operating systems. When a client computer is configured to use automatic addressing (DHCP), APIPA assigns a class B IP address from 169.254.0.0 to 169.254.255.255 to the client when a DHCP server is unavailable.

QUESTION 54:

A network administrator is configuring one distribution and five access switches which will be installed in a new building. Which of the following is the BEST physical location for the equipment?

1. The distribution switch in the IDF and the access switches in the MDF

2. The distribution switch in the MDF and the access switches in the IDF
3. All switches should be placed in the IDF to leave room in the MDF for servers
4. All switches should be placed in the MDF to leave room in the IDF for servers

Correct Answer(s): 2

Explanation:

Distribution switches should be placed in the Main Distribution Facility (MDF) and the access switches would be placed in the IDF closer to the end users.

QUESTION 55:

You are setting up uplink ports for multiple switches to communicate with one another. All of the VLANs should communicate from the designated server switch. Which of the following should be set on the uplink ports if VLAN 1 is not the management VLAN?

1. STP
2. 802.1q
3. Port security
4. 802.1x

Correct Answer(s): 1

Explanation:

Setting STP on the uplink ports will ensure that loops are not created.

QUESTION 56:

Which parameter must be adjusted to enable a jumbo frame on a network device?

1. MTU
2. TTL
3. Duplex
4. Speed

Correct Answer(s): 1

Explanation:

A jumbo frame is an Ethernet frame with a payload greater than the standard maximum transmission unit (MTU) of 1,500 bytes. Jumbo frames are used on local area networks that support at least 1 Gbps and can be as large as 9,000 bytes. By adjusting the MTU on a given network device's interface, you can enable or prevent jumbo frames from being used in the network.

QUESTION 57:

What benefit does network segmentation provide?

1. Security through isolation
2. Link aggregation
3. Packet flooding through all ports
4. High availability through redundancy

Correct Answer(s): 1

Explanation:

Network segmentation in computer networking is the act of splitting a computer network into subnetworks, each being a network segment. Advantages of such splitting are primarily for boosting performance and improving security through isolation.

QUESTION 58:

Max is a network technician who just terminated the ends on a new copper cable used between two legacy switches. When he connects the two switches together using the cable, they fail to establish a connection. What is MOST likely the issue?

1. The cable has exceeded bend radius limitations
2. The cable is a straight-through cable
3. The cable is a crossover cable
4. The cable has RJ-11 connectors instead of RJ-45

Correct Answer(s): 2

Explanation:

There are two types of cable, Straight-through and Crossover. In this instance, a crossover cable would need to be used to communicate with legacy switches since they won't support MDIX.

QUESTION 59:

A technician is troubleshooting a PC that is having intermittent connectivity issues. The technician notices that the STP cables pairs are not completely twisted near the connector. Which of the following issues may be experienced due to this?

1. Cross-talk
2. 568A/568B mismatch
3. Tx/Rx reverse
4. Split Pairs

Correct Answer(s): 1

Explanation:

Cross-talk can occur if the twisted pairs are not twisted sufficiently. The cable should be trimmed down and reterminated to prevent this issue.

QUESTION 60:

An organization wants to improve its ability to detect infiltration of servers in a DMZ. IPS/IDS solutions are currently located on the edge between DMZ and Untrust, and DMZ and Trust. Which of the following could increase visibility inside the DMZ?

1. Layer 7 firewall
2. Honeypot
3. NAC server
4. Host-based firewalls in the DMZ

Correct Answer(s): 1

Explanation:

Layer 7 firewalls are at the application layer. They allow you to choose your security at a more granular (almost undetectable) level.

QUESTION 61:

A wireless technician wants to configure a wireless network to identify itself to visitors by including the word "Guest" in the name. This wireless network needs to provide coverage to the entire building and will require 3 wireless access points working together to accomplish this level of coverage. What would allow users to identify the wireless network by its displayed name as a single network?

1. ESSID broadcast

2. ARP broadcast
3. BSSID broadcast
4. DHCP broadcast

Correct Answer(s): 1

Explanation:

With an ESSID (Extended Service Set), a wireless network can utilize multiple wireless access points (WAPs) that can broadcast a single network name for access by the clients. A BSSID (Basic Service Set) can only utilize a single WAP in each wireless network.

QUESTION 62:

Your office is located in a small office park and you are installing a new wireless network access point for your employees. The companies in the adjacent offices are using Wireless B/G/N routers in the 2.4 Ghz spectrum. Your security system is using the 5 Ghz spectrum, so you have purchased a 2.4 Ghz wireless access point to ensure you don't interfere with the security system. To maximize the distance between channels, which set of channels should you configure your WAP to use?

1. 1, 7, 13
2. 3, 6, 9
3. 2, 6, 10
4. 1, 6, 11

Correct Answer(s): 4

Explanation:

Wireless access points should always be configured with channels 1, 6, or 11 to maximize the distance between channels and prevent overlaps.

QUESTION 63:

After installing some new switches in your network, you notice that a looping problem has begun to occur. You contact the manufacturer's technical support for the switches you purchased and they recommended that you enable 802.1d. Which of the following BEST represents why the manufacturer suggested this?

1. It is a version of spanning tree that uses BPDU to detect problems
2. It is a regular version of port mirroring that uses hello packets to detect loops
3. It is a simple version of port mirroring tree that uses BPDU to detect problems

4. It is a rapid version or port mirroring that uses BPDU to detect problems

Correct Answer(s): 1

Explanation:

The IEEE 802.1d standard refers to the Spanning Tree Protocol (STP). The main purpose of STP is to ensure that you do not create loops when you have redundant paths in your network. The other options are focused on port mirroring, which is not covered by this question.

QUESTION 64:

What is true concerning jumbo frames?

1. They are commonly used on a SAN
2. Their MTU size is less than 1500
3. They are commonly used with a NAS
4. They are commonly used with DHCP

Correct Answer(s): 1

Explanation:

Jumbo frames are Ethernet frames whose MTU is greater than 1500. To increase performance, you should use jumbo frames only when you have a dedicated network or VLAN, and you can configure an MTU of 9000 on all equipment. Because of this, jumbo frames are most commonly used in a separate SAN (storage area network).

QUESTION 65:

A technician has attempted to optimize the network but some segments are still reporting poor performance. What issue should the technician look at?

1. Switch incorrectly set to full duplex
2. Conflicting IP addresses
3. Packet bottlenecks
4. IP address scope depletion

Correct Answer(s): 3

Explanation:

A bottleneck occurs when bandwidth is unable to accommodate large amounts of system data at designated data transfer rate speed, typically caused by TCP/IP data interruption or other performance issues.

QUESTION 66:

You are working as a network technician and have been asked to troubleshoot an issue with a workstation. You have just established a theory of probable cause. Which of the following steps should you perform NEXT?

1. Identify the problem
2. Verify full system functionality
3. Test the theory to determine cause
4. Implement the solution or escalate as necessary

Correct Answer(s): 3

Explanation:

There are 7 steps to the troubleshooting methodology used in Network+. (1) Identify the problem. (2) Establish a theory of probable cause. (3) Test the theory to determine the cause. (4) Establish a plan of action to resolve the problem and identify potential effects. (5) Implement the solution or escalate as necessary. (6) Verify full system functionality and if applicable implement preventative measures. (7) Document findings, actions, and outcomes.

QUESTION 67:

You are installing a new LAN in a building your company just purchased. The building is older, but your company has decided to install a brand new Cat6a network in it before moving in. You are trying to determine whether to purchase plenum or PVC cabling. Which environment condition should be considered prior to making the purchase?

1. Workstation models
2. Window placement
3. Floor composition
4. Ceiling air flow condition

Correct Answer(s): 4

Explanation:

In a large building, the 'plenum' is the space between floors used to circulate the air conditioning ductwork, piping, electrical, and network cables throughout the building. This space is also an ideal place to run computer network cabling. However, in the event of fire in the building, the network cables can be very hazardous as they create a noxious gas when burnt. If you have a plenum area in the ceiling with excellent airflow, you may be able to use PVC cables instead (which are cheaper). Generally, though, if you are going to run your cables in a plenum area (as opposed to open cable trays), then you want to use plenum rated cables.

QUESTION 68:

Which type of a security measure is used to control access to an area by using a retina scan?

1. Two-factor authentication
2. Biometric
3. Cipher locks
4. Optical reader

Correct Answer(s): 2

Explanation:

Retina scans are considered a biometric control. Other biometric controls contains fingerprint readers and facial scanners.

QUESTION 69:

A network technician must replace a network interface card on a server. The server currently uses a multimode fiber to uplink a fiber switch. Which of the following types of NICs should the technician install on the server?

1. 1000base-LR
2. 1000Base-FX
3. 1000Base-T
4. 10GBase-SR

Correct Answer(s): 4

Explanation:

10Gbase-SR is a 10 Gigabit Ethernet LAN standard for operation over multi-mode fiber optic cable and short wavelength signaling. Remember, for the exam, "S is not single", meaning the ones that has a Base-S as part of its name designates it as a multimode fiber cable.

QUESTION 70:

As part of unified communications services, QoS must be implemented to provide support for DSCP and CoS. Which of the following OSI layers does QoS operate within?

1. Layer 1
2. Layer 2
3. Layer 4
4. Layer 5

Correct Answer(s): 2

Explanation:

DSCP is a layer 3 packet and it is the most commonly used value for QoS of an IP packet (as it gives lots of flexibility). CoS, on the other hand, is a layer 2 packet. Based on the options given, only Layer 2 is correct.

QUESTION 71:

Your company wants to create highly-available data centers. Which of the following will allow the company to continue to maintain an Internet presence at all sites in the event that the WAN connection at their own site goes down?

1. Load balancer
2. VRRP
3. OSPF
4. BGP

Correct Answer(s): 4

Explanation:

If a WAN link goes down, BGP will route data through another WAN link if redundant WAN links are available.

QUESTION 72:

You have been asked by a client to provide their local office with the BEST solution for a wireless network based on their requirements. The client has stated that their users will need a wireless network that provides a maximum of 54 Mbps of bandwidth and operates in the 2.4Ghz frequency band. Which of the following types of wireless network should you install to meet their needs?

1. 802.11a
2. 802.11b
3. 802.11g
4. 802.11ac

Correct Answer(s): 3

Explanation:

802.11g provides transmission over short distances at up to 54 Mbps in the 2.4 GHz band. It's also backwards compatible with 802.11b (which only operates at 11 Mbps). While a 802.11ac network would be the faster solution, it does not operate in the 2.4 Ghz frequency band. 802.11a operates in the 5 GHz frequency band at up to 54 Mbps.

QUESTION 73:

What is used to define how much bandwidth can be used by various protocols on the network?

1. Traffic shaping
2. High availability
3. Load balancing
4. Fault tolerance

Correct Answer(s): 1

Explanation:

Traffic shaping, also known as packet shaping, is the manipulation and prioritization of network traffic to reduce the impact of heavy users or machines from affecting other users.

QUESTION 74:

You are troubleshooting a SQL server on the network. It has been unable to perform an uncompressed backup of the database because it needs several terabytes of disk space available. Which of the following devices should you install in order to have the MOST cost efficient backup solution?

1. iSCSI scan
2. FCoE SAN
3. NAS
4. USB flash drive

Correct Answer(s): 3

Explanation:

A NAS is a Network Attached Storage device, typically a bunch of cheap hard disks and usually arranged in a RAID consisting of either SAS (serial attached SCSI) or SATA disks just like the ones in most desktops.

QUESTION 75:

An administrator has configured a new 100Mbps WAN circuit, but speed testing shows poor performance when downloading large files. The download initially reaches close to 100Mbps but begins to drop and show spikes in the download speeds over time. The administrator checks the router interface and sees the following: Router01# show interface eth1/1 GigabitEthernet1/1 is up, line is up Hardware is GigabitEthernet, address is FF12.CDEA.1426 Configured speed auto, actual 1Gbit, configured duplex fdx, actual fdx Member of L2 VLAN 1, port is untagged, port state is forwarding Which of the following is the best solution to resolve this issue?

1. Shutdown and then re-enable this interface
2. Reset the statistics counter for this interface
3. Remove default 802.1q tag and set to server VLAN
4. Apply egress port rate-shaping

Correct Answer(s): 3

Explanation:

Since the VLAN port is untagged, it can be slowing down performance. It is recommended to remove the default VLAN tag and setup a server VLAN to increase performance.

Practice Exam #6

QUESTION 1:

A client is concerned about a hacker compromising a network in order to gain access to confidential research data. What could be implemented to redirect any attackers on the network?

1. DMZ
2. Content filter
3. Botnet
4. Honeypot

Correct Answer(s): 4

Explanation:

A honeypot is a computer security mechanism set to detect, deflect, or in some manner counteract attempts at unauthorized use of information systems. Generally, a honeypot consists of data that appears to be a legitimate part of the site, but is actually isolated and monitored, and seems to contain information or a resource of value to attackers, who are then blocked.

QUESTION 2:

After upgrading a fiber link from 1Gbps, a network technician ran a speed test of the link. The test shows the link is not operating at full speed and connectivity is intermittent. The two buildings are 1,476ft (450m) apart and are connected using CM4 fiber and 10G SR SFPs. The fiber runs through the electrical and boiler rooms of each building. Which of the following is the MOST likely cause of the connectivity issues?

1. The wrong SFPs are being used
2. There is interference from the electrical room
3. CM1 fiber should be used instead
4. There is heat from the boiler room

Correct Answer(s): 1

Explanation:

The process of elimination allows us to drop out interference from the electrical room and heat from the boiler room as the heat definitely doesn't cause connectivity issues. There's not much information on the CM1 fiber, however, SFPs will work but will not work in a GBIC port intended for SFP+.

QUESTION 3:

A network administrator is noticing slow response times from the server to hosts on the network. After adding several new hosts, the administrator realizes that CSMA/CD results in network slowness due to congestion at the server NIC. What should the network administrator do?

1. Add a honeypot to reduce traffic to the server
2. Update the Ethernet drivers to use 802.3
3. Add additional network cards to the server
4. Disable CSMA/CD on the network

Correct Answer(s): 3

Explanation:

Adding dual NICs to the server can increase the bandwidth at the server and minimize congestion.

QUESTION 4:

A network technician is diligent about maintaining all system servers at the most current service pack level available. After performing upgrades, users experience issues with server-based applications. Which of the following should be used to prevent issues in the future?

1. Configure an automated patching server
2. Virtualize the servers and take daily snapshots
3. Configure a honeypot for application testing
4. Configure a test lab for updates

Correct Answer(s): 4

Explanation:

To prevent the service pack issues, make sure to validate them in a test/lab environment first before going ahead and applying a new Service Pack in your production environment. While using an automated patching server is a good idea, no patches should be deployed prior to being tested in a lab first.

QUESTION 5:

A firewall technician configures a firewall in order to allow HTTP traffic as follows:
Source IP   Zone   Dest IP   Zone   Port   ActionAny   Untrust   Any
DMZ   80   Allow The organization should upgrade to what technology to prevent unauthorized traffic from traversing the firewall?

1. HTTPS
2. Stateless packet inspection
3. Intrusion detection system
4. Application aware firewall

Correct Answer(s): 4

Explanation:

Application aware firewall can analyze and verify protocols all the way up to layer 7 of the OSI reference model. It has the advantage to be aware of the details at the application layer. Since we desired to allow HTTP traffic, we must deal with the traffic at the application layer. This will prevent an attacker from sending SSH traffic over port 80, for example. By using an application aware firewall, only HTTP traffic will be allowed over port 80.

QUESTION 6:

What network device uses ACLs to prevent unauthorized access into company systems?

1. IDS
2. Firewall
3. Content filter
4. Load balancer

Correct Answer(s): 2

Explanation:

A firewall is a network security device which is designed to prevent systems or traffic from unauthorized access. An ACL is a list that shows which traffic or devices should be allowed into or denied from accessing the network.

QUESTION 7:

You have just moved into a new condo in a large building. Your wireless network is acting strangely so you are worried that it may be due to interference from the numerous other wireless networks in the building since each apartment has its own wireless access point. You want to determine what wireless signals are within the walls of your apartment and their relative strength. What technique should you utilize to determine whether the nearby wireless networks are causing interference with your own Wifi network?

1. Conduct a vulnerability scan
2. Perform wardriving around your neighborhood

3. Perform a bandwidth test
4. Conduct a site survey within your apartment

Correct Answer(s): 4

Explanation:

If you suspect interference within your apartment or other personal spaces, you should conduct a site survey to identify what wireless signals are emanating into your apartment and how strong their signals are. This will allow you to choose the least used frequency/channel to increase your own signal strength and reduce the interference to your own wireless network.

QUESTION 8:

A software company is meeting with a car manufacturer to finalize discussions. In the signed document, the software company will provide the latest versions of its mapping application suite for the car manufacturer's next generation of cars. In return, the car manufacturer will provide three specific vehicle analytics to the software company to enhance the software company's mapping application suite. The software company can offer its enhanced mapping application to other car manufacturers but must pay the car manufacturer a royalty. Which of the following BEST describes the document used in this scenario?

1. MSA
2. SLA
3. MOU
4. AUP

Correct Answer(s): 3

Explanation:

MOU is a memorandum of understanding. This is the most accurate description based on the choices given.

QUESTION 9:

A disgruntled employee executes a man-in-the-middle attack on the company network. Layer 2 traffic destined for the gateway is redirected to the employee's computer. This type of attack is an example of:

1. ARP cache poisoning
2. IP spoofing
3. Amplified DNS attack
4. Evil twin

Correct Answer(s): 1

Explanation:

ARP poisoning reroutes data and allows an attacker to intercept packets of data intended for another recipient. ARP attacks can be sent from any host on the local area network and the goal is to associate the host so that any traffic meant for something else will instead go directly to the attacker's PC.

QUESTION 10:

Which storage network technology utilizes file-level storage to function properly?

1. iSCSI
2. FCoE
3. NAS
4. SAN

Correct Answer(s): 3

Explanation:

A NAS uses file-level storage, while the others all use block-level storage. Block-level storage is a type of storage commonly deployed by larger businesses and enterprises in storage area networks (SANs) and similar large-scale storage systems. Each block in a block-level storage system can be controlled as an individual hard drive, and the blocks are managed by a server operating system. Block-level storage protocols like iSCSI, Fibre Channel and FCoE (Fibre Channel over Ethernet) are utilized to make the storage blocks visible and accessible by the server-based operating system.

QUESTION 11:

A network technician is selecting the best way to protect a branch office from as many different threats from the Internet as possible using a single device. Which of the following should meet these requirements?

1. Configure a network-based firewall
2. Configure a firewall with UTM
3. Configure a host-based firewall
4. Configure a host-based intrusion detection system

Correct Answer(s): 2

Explanation:

Since this is a branch office and you want to protect yourself from as many threats as possible, using a Unified Threat Management firewall would be best. It will protect you from the most things using a single device. A network-based firewall protects everything on the other side of the Internet (your network). Host-based firewalls are great too but the network-based firewall is configured once to protect all devices.

QUESTION 12:

Today, your company's network started to experience network connectivity issues for various workstations around the company. As you begin troubleshooting, you identify that all the workstations receive their connectivity from a single switch on the 3rd floor of the office building. You start searching the 3rd floor for the cause of this issue and find a small wired router plugged into a network jack in the office of the Sales manager. From this small wired router, he has connected his workstation and a small Smart TV so he can watch Netflix while working. You ask the sales manager when he brought in the new router and he says he just hooked it up this morning. What type of issue did the sales manager accidentally introduced into the network by installing the router?

1. Evil twin
2. VLAN mismatch
3. Network loop
4. Rogue DHCP server

Correct Answer(s): 4

Explanation:

Routers usually contain their own DHCP servers. When the sales manager installed the wired router, he inadvertently introduced a secondary DHCP server into the network. This could cause the same IP addresses to be assigned to two different workstations, resulting in connectivity issues for those workstations. Had the sales manager installed a simple hub or switch, this would not have caused any issues. Because this is a wired router, it cannot be an evil twin since evil twins are wireless access points. Also, we have no indication of a VLAN mismatch, since this would only affect the workstations connected to this router. Similarly, we have no indication of a network loop, so this network might already be implementing good practices by utilizing a STP to prevent them.

QUESTION 13:

Your company has just installed a brand new email server, but during the initial tests you determined that the server is unable to send emails to another server. You decided to check the firewall's ACL to see if the server's outgoing email is being blocked. Which of the following ports should you ensure is open and not blocked by the firewall?

1. 143
2. 995
3. 25
4. 110

Correct Answer(s): 3

Explanation:

Port 25 is the designated port for the Simple Mail Transfer Protocol. SMTP is used for outbound email, including mail relay functionality.

QUESTION 14:

The network install is failing redundancy testing at the MDF. The traffic being transported is a mixture of multicast and unicast signals. Which of the following devices would BEST handle the rerouting caused by the disruption of service?

1. Layer 3 switch
2. Proxy server
3. Layer 2 switch
4. Smart hub

Correct Answer(s): 1

Explanation:

A layer 3 switch is the best option because in addition to its capability of broadcast traffic reduction, it provides fault isolation and simplified security management. This is achieved through the use of IP address information to make routing decisions when managing traffic between LANs.

QUESTION 15:

During a business trip, Bobby connects to the wireless network at the hotel to send emails to some of his clients. The next day, Bobby notices that additional emails have been sent out from his account without consent. Which of the following protocols was MOST likely used to compromise the Bobby's email password utilizing a network sniffer?

1. SSL
2. HTTP
3. TFTP
4. DNS

Correct Answer(s): 2

Explanation:

HTTP is an unsecured protocol and information is passed without encryption. If the user signed into their webmail over HTTP instead of HTTPS, a network sniffer could compromise the username and password. Additionally, if the user was using an email client, then the SMTP connection could have been compromised, but since that wasn't an option in this question, we must assume Bobby used a webmail client over HTTP instead.

QUESTION 16:

A desktop computer is connected to the network and receives an APIPA address but is unable to reach the VLAN gateway of 10.10.100.254. Other PCs in the VLAN subnet are able to reach the Internet. What is the MOST likely source of the problem?

1. 802.1q is configured on the switch port
2. APIPA has been misconfigured on the VLAN
3. Bad SFP in the PC's 10/100 NIC
4. OS updates have not been installed

Correct Answer(s): 1

Explanation:

APIPA addresses are self-configured and are used when the client is unable to get proper IP configuration from a DHCP server. One possible source of this problem is a misconfigured switch port that the computer is connected to. The 802.1q protocol is used to configure VLAN trunking and should be configured on the trunk port, not the on switch port.

QUESTION 17:

A technician is troubleshooting a desktop connectivity issue. The technician believes a static ARP may be causing the problem. What should the technician do NEXT according to the network troubleshooting methodology?

1. Remove the ARP entry on the user's desktop
2. Identify a suitable time to resolve the issue on the affected desktop
3. Duplicate the issue in a lab by removing the ARP entry
4. Document the findings and provide a plan of action

Correct Answer(s): 1

Explanation:

Based on the troubleshooting methodology, once you have come up with a probable cause (the static ARP entry), you should try to test your hypothesis. Since this issue has already cause the workstation to not be able to communicate, the best way to test your theory would be to remove the static ARP entry and see if the issue is resolved. If this doesn't fix the issue, you would need to then come up with a new hypothesis, and test it as well.

QUESTION 18:

Your company just moved into a beautiful new building. The building has been built with large glass windows that cover most of the walls and ceiling to provide natural light to be visible throughout the offices. You have noticed that your cell phone gets really poor cellular connectivity when inside the building. What is the MOST likely cause of the poor cellular service within the building?

1. Frequency mismatch
2. Channel overlap
3. Absorption
4. Reflection

Correct Answer(s): 4

Explanation:

A cellular signal is comprised of radio waves. Just like light, radio waves can bounce off of certain surfaces and materials. Metal and glass are considered highly reflective materials which can cause poor cellular service and connectivity within office buildings that use intricately designed glass walls and ceilings. If a large amount of reflection occurs, signals can be weakened and also cause interference at the receiver's device.

QUESTION 19:

When a switch has multiple paths to reach the root bridge, what state is the port with the LEAST desirable path placed by the spanning tree protocol?

1. Forwarding

2. Bonding
3. Blocking
4. Listening

Correct Answer(s): 3

Explanation:

Blocking is the state in the spanning tree protocol that prevents looping in the network.

QUESTION 20:

Users are reporting extreme slowness across the network every Friday. What should the network technician review first to narrow down the root cause of the problem?

1. Baseline
2. Bottleneck
3. Utilization
4. Link status

Correct Answer(s): 3

Explanation:

Reviewing the network utilization can help the technician identify why the slowness is being experienced every Friday, such as users placing additional load on the network by streaming videos or something similar.

QUESTION 21:

(This is a simulated Performance-Based Question.)

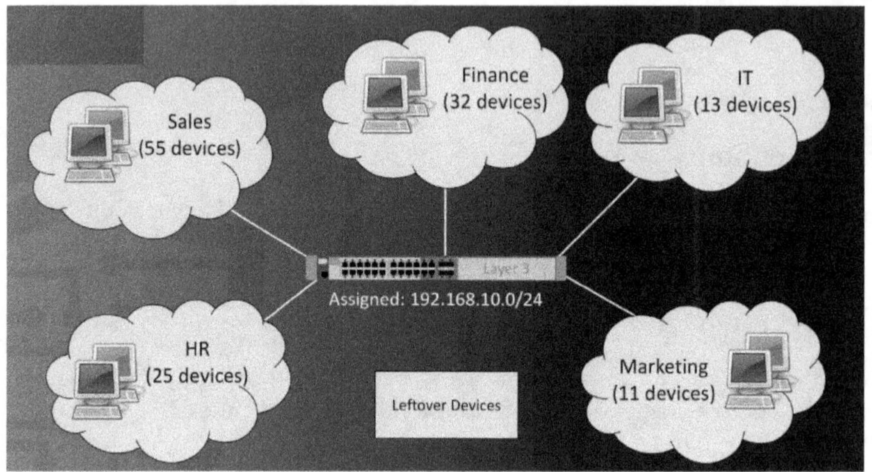

The company's corporate headquarters provided your branch office a portion of their Class C subnet to use at a new office location. You must allocate the minimum number of addresses using CIDR notation in order to accommodate each department's needs. You have finished providing the minimum number of addresses using CIDR notation to each of the departments listed. Calculate the number of leftover IP addresses. What is the correct CIDR notation to use to represent the available number of leftover IP addresses?

    1.   /25
    2.   /26
    3.   /27
    4.   /28
    5.   /29
    6.   /30

Correct Answer(s): 2

Explanation:

For this question, you began with a /24 network (256 total IPs, with 254 usable IPs). The Sales department needs 55 usable IPs, so you should have used a /26 (62 usable IPs, 64 total IPs). The Finance department needs 32 usable IPs, so you should have used a /26 (62 usable IPs, 64 total IPs). The IT department needs 13 usable IPs, so you should have used a /28 (14 usable IPs, 16 total IPs). The HR department needs 25 usable IPs, so you should have used a /27 (30 usable IPs, 32 total IPs). The Marketing department needs 11 usable IPs, so you should have used a /28 (14 usable IPs, 16 total IPs). So, we have already used up many of the original /24 (256 total

IPs). If we take $256 - 64 - 64 - 16 - 32 - 16$, we find that we have 64 IPs left (or a /26). This gives us the answer for the unused portion of the IP space for this question.

QUESTION 22:

(This is a simulated Performance-Based Question.) After some recent changes to the network, several users are complaining that they are unable to access the servers. You have been provided with the Internet Protocol Version 4 (IPv4) Properties for PC1, PC2, PC3, and PC4.

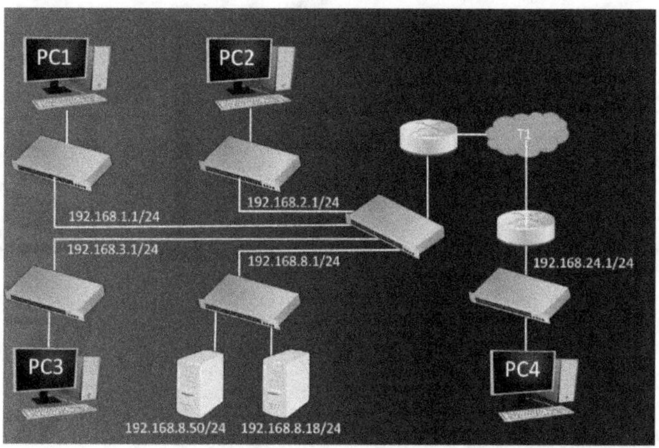

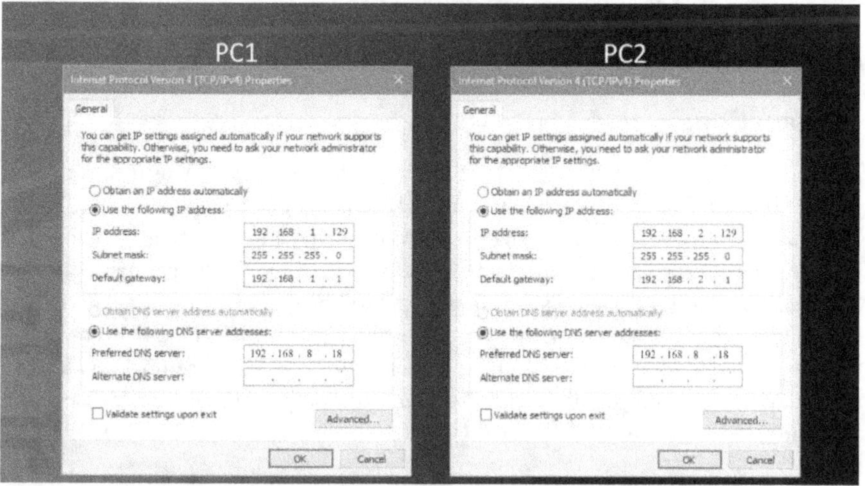

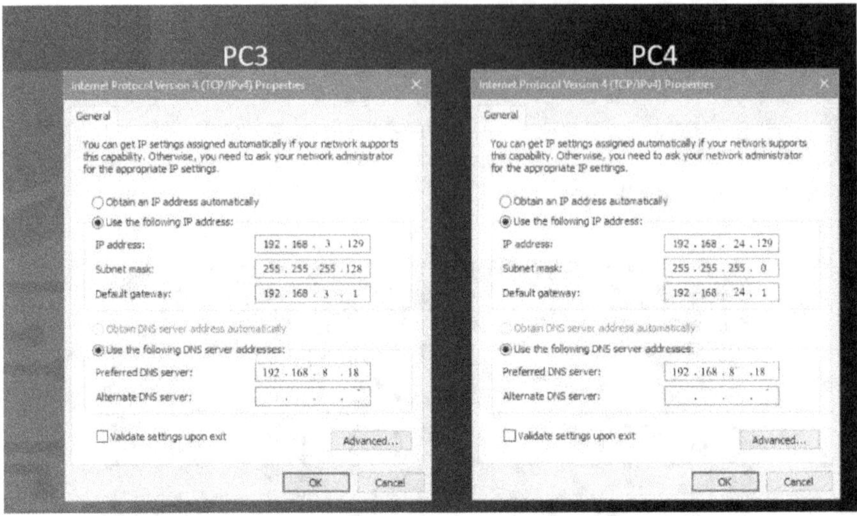

Which of the following actions should you perform to fix the issue and ensure the computers can communicate with the servers again?

1. Change PC3's IP address to 192.168.3.200
2. Change PC4's subnet mask to 255.255.255.128
3. Change PC3's subnet mask to 255.255.255.0
4. Change the DNS server on PC1, PC2, PC3, and PC4 to Google DNS (8.8.8.8)

Correct Answer(s): 3

Explanation:

PC3's IP is 192.168.3.129, but its subnet mask is 255.255.255.128. This means that the 192.168.3.0/24 network is split into two (192.168.3.0/25 and 192.168.3.128/25). The current configuration means that PC3 is not on the same subnet as its default gateway, and is causing the connectivity issue. If you change the subnet mask to 255.255.255.0, both PC3 and its default gateway will be on the same subnet and connectivity will be restored. (If you get a question like this on exam day, you will only get the network diagram at first. As you click on each PC, its settings will be shown as a popup and you will be able to change the settings using your mouse and keyboard.)

QUESTION 23:

(This is a simulated Performance-Based Question.)

Which of the following is the correct order of the following Fiber Connectors shown?

1. FC, LC (single), LC (duplex), SC, ST
2. SC, ST, FC, LC (single), LC (duplex)
3. ST, SC, LC (single), LC (duplex), FC
4. LC (single), LC (duplex), FC, ST, SC

Correct Answer(s): 3

Explanation:

The correct order of the Fiber connections shown is ST, SC, LC (single), LC (duplex), and FC. If this was a real question on the exam, you would have the words provided in a list, and you would drag them below the appropriate fiber connector's drawing.

QUESTION 24:

(This is a simulated Performance-Based Question.)

Computer to Computer

What type of cable would you use to connect a computer to a computer?

1. Crossover
2. RG-6
3. Rollover
4. RS-232
5. Straight-through

Correct Answer(s): 1

Explanation:

When you connect two computers together directly without a hub or switch between them, you must use a crossover cable to switch the transmit and receive pins. If this was a real question on the exam, you would have the words provided in a list, and you would drag them below the appropriate drawing.

QUESTION 25:

(This is a simulated Performance-Based Question.) What ports do SMTP and SNMP utilize?

1. 23, 25
2. 161, 443
3. 445, 3389
4. 25, 161

Correct Answer(s): 4

Explanation:

SMTP (Simple Mail Transfer Protocol) uses port 25. SNMP (Simple Network Management Protocol) uses port 161. If this was a question on the real exam, you would see a list of ports on one side and a list of protocols on the other, and you would drag and drop each one to match them up.

QUESTION 26:

Last night, your company's system administrators conducted a server upgrade. This morning, several users are having issues accessing the company's share drive on the network. You have been asked to troubleshoot the problem. What document should you look at first to create a probable theory for the cause of the issue?

1. Change management documentation
2. Release notes for the server software
3. Physical network diagram

4. Cable management plan

Correct Answer(s): 1

Explanation:

Since everything worked before the server upgrade and doesn't now, it would be a good idea to first look at the change management documentation that authorized the change/upgrade. This should include the specific details of what was changed and what things may have been affected by the change. This is the best place to start when determining what changed since yesterday.

QUESTION 27:

Dion Training Solutions is launching their brand new website. The website needs to be continually accessible to our students and reachable 24x7. Which networking concept would BEST ensure that the website remains up at all times?

1. Snapshots
2. Warm site
3. Cold site
4. High availability

Correct Answer(s): 4

Explanation:

High availability is a concept that uses redundant technologies and processes to ensure that a system is up and accessible to the end users at all times. Snapshots, warm sites, and cold sites may be useful for recovering from a disaster-type event, but they will not ensure high availability.

QUESTION 28:

Which of the following concepts is the MOST important for a company's long-term health in the event of a disaster?

1. Vulnerability scanning
2. Implementing acceptable use policy
3. Offsite backups
4. Uninterruptible power supplies

Correct Answer(s): 3

Explanation:

In case of a disaster, you must protect your data. Some of the most common strategies for data protection include backups made to tape and sent off site at regular intervals. All of the other options are good, too, but the MOST important is a good backup copy of your company's data.

QUESTION 29:

You work for a small company that wants to add a share drive to their network. They are looking for a simple solution that will easily integrate into the existing network, will be easy to configure, and can share files with all the network clients over TCP/IP. Which of the following is the BEST recommended storage solution for this network?

1. Fibre Channel
2. NAS
3. iSCSI
4. FCOE

Correct Answer(s): 2

Explanation:

A network-attached storage (NAS) device is a self-contained computer that connects to a home or business network and can share files over TCP/IP. It is a rapidly growing choice for data storage and can provide data access to numerous users on a network. A NAS consists of hard disk for storage of files and usually utilizes a RAID system for redundancy and/or performance.

QUESTION 30:

After an employee connected one of the switch ports on a SOHO router to the wall jack in the office, other employees in the building started losing network connectivity. Which of the following could be implemented on the company's switch to prevent this type of loss of connection?

1. Loop prevention
2. ARP inspections
3. DHCP snooping
4. MAC address filtering

Correct Answer(s): 1

Explanation:

It appears the connection of the SOHO router to the company network has caused a loop in the network, causing the loss of connectivity to other users. If the company network implements a loop prevention mechanism, such as Spanning Tree Protocol (STP), this will prevent a loop from occurring.

QUESTION 31:

During a recent penetration test, it was discovered that your company's wireless network can be reached from the parking lot. The Chief Security Officer has submitted a change request to your network engineering team to solve this issue because he wants to ensure that the wireless network is only accessible from within the building. Based on these requirements, which of the following settings should be changed to ensure the wireless signal doesn't extend beyond the interior of your building while maintaining a high level of availability to your users?

1. Power level
2. Channel
3. Frequency
4. Encryption

Correct Answer(s): 1

Explanation:

The power level should be reduced for the radio transmitted in the wireless access points. With a reduced power level, the signal will not travel as far and this can ensure the signal remains within the interior of the building only. The other options, if changed, would affect the availability of the network to the currently configured users and their devices.

QUESTION 32:

A technician wants to implement a network for testing remote devices before allowing them to connect to the corporate network. What could the technician implement to meet this requirement?

1. High availability
2. MAN network
3. Quarantine
4. Honeynet

Correct Answer(s): 3

Explanation:

Quarantine is where devices that do not meet the standards for the regular network can be placed. In this area, they can be checked before connecting to the main network.

QUESTION 33:

A company is setting up a brand new server room and would like to keep the cabling infrastructure out of sight but still accessible to the network administrators. Infrastructure cost is not an issue. Which of the following should be installed to meet the requirements?

1. Conduit
2. Cable trays
3. Patch panels
4. Raised floor

Correct Answer(s): 4

Explanation:

Raised floors allow the cabling to be placed under the floor, but still accessible to the network administrators.

QUESTION 34:

Company policies require that all network infrastructure devices send system level information to a centralized server. Which of the following should be implemented to ensure the network administrator can review device error information from one central location?

1. TACACS+ server
2. Single sign-on
3. Syslog server
4. Wifi analyzer

Correct Answer(s): 3

Explanation:

Syslog is a protocol designed to send log entries generated by a device or process called a facility across an IP network to a message collector, called a syslog server. A syslog message consists of an error code and the severity of the error. A syslog server would enable the network administrator to view device error information from a central location.

QUESTION 35:

A common technique used by malicious individuals to perform a man-in-the-middle attack on a wireless network is:

1.   ARP cache poisoning
2.   Amplified DNS attacks
3.   Sessions hijacking
4.   Creating an evil twin

Correct Answer(s): 4

Explanation:

Evil Twin access points are the most common way to perform a man-in-the-middle attack on a wireless network.

QUESTION 36:

A network administrator is following the best practices to implement firewalls, patch management, and policies on his network. Which of the following should be performed to verify that the security controls are in place?

1.   Penetration testing
2.   AAA authentication testing
3.   Disaster recovery testing
4.   Single point of failure testing

Correct Answer(s): 1

Explanation:

Penetration testing (also called pen testing) is the practice of testing a computer system, network, or web application in order to find vulnerabilities that an attacker could exploit. It can be used to ensure all security controls are properly configured and in place.

QUESTION 37:

Dion Training has just installed a new web server and created an A record for DionTraining.com. When users try entering www.DionTraining.com, though, they get an error. You tell their network administrator that the problem is because he forgot to add the appropriate DNS record to create an alias for www to the root of the domain. Which type of DNS record should be added to fix this issue?

1. PTR
2. NS
3. CNAME
4. AAAA

Correct Answer(s): 3

Explanation:

CNAME records can be used to alias one name to another. CNAME stands for Canonical Name. A common example is when you have both diontraining.com and www.diontraining.com pointing to the same application and hosted by the same server.

QUESTION 38:

You typed IPCONFIG at the command prompt and find out your IP is 192.168.1.24. You then go to Google.com and search for "what is my IP", and it returns a value of 35.25.52.11. How do you explain the different values for the IP addresses?

1. This is caused by the way traffic is routed over the internet
2. This is caused by how a switch handles IP addresses
3. This is caused because of the way routers handle IP addresses
4. This occurs because your network uses a private IP address internal but a public IP address over the internet

Correct Answer(s): 4

Explanation:

Your computer network is using a private IP address for machines within the network and assigns a public IP address for traffic being routed over the network. Most small office home office (SOHO) networks utilize a single public IP for all of their devices and use a technique known as NAT to associate the public IP with each internal client's private IP when needed.

QUESTION 39:

An administrator is told they need to set up a space in the breakroom where employees can relax. So, the administrator sets up several televisions with interconnected video game systems in the breakroom. What type of network did the administrator setup?

1.   CAN
2.   MAN
3.   WAN
4.   LAN

Correct Answer(s): 4

Explanation:

Since this gaming network is within one room, it is considered a LAN. All the other answers require a larger geographical area.

QUESTION 40:

Which of the following is used to connect Cat5e or above networks in an MDF or IDF?

1.   66 block
2.   110 block
3.   F-connector
4.   RJ-11

Correct Answer(s): 2

Explanation:

A 110 block is a type of punch block used to terminate runs of on-premises wiring in a structured cabling system. The designation 110 is also used to describe a type of insulation displacement contact (IDC) connector used to terminate twisted pair cables, which uses a punch-down tool similar to the older 66 block. 110 blocks provide more spacing between the terminals and are designed for Cat 5 networks to eliminate crosstalk between the cables.

QUESTION 41:

Which network device operates at Layer 1?

1.   Hub
2.   Bridge
3.   Router
4.   Firewall

Correct Answer(s): 1

Explanation:

A hub is a layer 1 device and operates at the physical layer. Cables, hubs, repeaters, and wireless access points are all examples of layer 1, or physical layer, devices.

QUESTION 42:

You have been asked to connect a laptop directly to a router in order to gain access to the internet. Unfortunately, this router is old and doesn't support MDIX on its ports. What type of cable should you use to connect the computer to the router?

1. Console
2. Rollover
3. Crossover
4. Patch

Correct Answer(s): 3

Explanation:

Since you are connecting two DTE (Data Terminating Equipment) devices and the router doesn't support MDIX, you will need a crossover cable to allow the computer and router to communicate. If you instead connected a switch (Data Communication Equipment) in between these two devices, then you could use a patch or straight-through cable instead.

QUESTION 43:

Which of the following communication technologies are used by video conferencing systems to synchronize video streams and reduce bandwidth being sent by a central location to subscribed devices?

1. Anycast
2. Unicast
3. CoS
4. Multicast

Correct Answer(s): 4

Explanation:

Multicasting is a technique used for a one-to-many communication over an IP network. In this example, the central location sends a signal to subscribed devices. It reduces bandwidth as the source only has to send the signal once, which is then received by multiple hosts simultaneously. Multicast is supported by both IPv4 and IPv6.

QUESTION 44:

There are two switches connected using both a CAT6 cable and a CAT5e cable. Which type of problem might occur with this setup?

1. Missing route
2. Auto sensing ports
3. Improper cable types
4. Switching loop

Correct Answer(s): 4

Explanation:

A switching loop is when there is more than one Layer 2 path between two endpoints. This can be prevented by using the STP (Spanning Tree Protocol).

QUESTION 45:

A client reports that half of the marketing department is unable to access network resources. The technician determines that the switch has failed and needs replacement. What would be the MOST helpful in regaining connectivity?

1. VLAN configuration
2. Network Diagram
3. Configuration backup
4. Router image

Correct Answer(s): 3

Explanation:

If you have a configuration backup of the switch, a new piece of hardware (new switch) can be installed quickly and the configuration can be restored to the new switch.

QUESTION 46:

Which type of antenna broadcasts an RF signal in a specific direction with a narrow path?

1. Omni-directional
2. Unidirectional

3. Patch
4. Bi-directional

Correct Answer(s): 2

Explanation:

Unidirectional is one direction. It focuses the broadcasting from the antenna in a single direction instead of all directions, focusing the transmission and making the signal stronger. A specific type of unidirectional antenna is known as a Yagi antenna, and this may be a term you may also see used on the Network+ certification exam.

QUESTION 47:

A technician has been troubleshooting a network problem, has determined the most likely cause of the issue, and implemented a solution. What is the NEXT step to be taken?

1. Document the findings, actions, and outcomes
2. Duplicate the problem if possible
3. Verify system functionality
4. Make an archival backup

Correct Answer(s): 3

Explanation:

Verifying system functionality occurs directly after the implementation of a solution. It is to ensure that your plan of action and your theory did in fact fix the problem. Documenting findings is the final step taken AFTER verifying the system.

QUESTION 48:

The service desk has received a large number of calls this morning complaining about how slow the network is responding when trying to connect to the internet. You are currently at one of the user's workstations and conducted a ping to Google.com, but the results showed that the response time was too slow and there was too much latency in the route between the workstation and Google.com. You then attempted to ping some of the network printers and other local servers on the network. The results showed acceptable response times. What should you try to do NEXT?

1. Reboot the email server
2. Scan the user's workstation for malware
3. Replace the cable between the user's workstation and the wall jack
4. Check the change control system to determine if any networking equipment was recently replaced

Correct Answer(s): 4

Explanation:

Since the ping command showed acceptable results when testing internally, you can assume the user's cable and workstation are not the issue. Also, the scenario never mentioned an email server, so rebooting that would not solve anything. Instead, you should try to identify what has changed since yesterday. By checking what has changed through the change control system, you can identify possible issues. Generally, if everything was fine yesterday, and it doesn't work right today, you should ask yourself, "what changed?"

QUESTION 49:

Various hypervisor guests are configured to use different VLANs in the same virtualization environment through what device?

1. Virtual router
2. Virtual firewall
3. NIC teaming
4. Virtual switch

Correct Answer(s): 4

Explanation:

Virtual switches can act like real switches, but are configured in the Hyper-V environment.

QUESTION 50:

It has been determined by network operations that there is a severe bottleneck on the company's mesh topology network. The field technician has chosen to use log management and found that one router is making routing decisions slower than the others on the network. What is this an example of?

1. Network device power issues
2. Network device CPU issues
3. Storage area network issues
4. Delayed responses from RADIUS

Correct Answer(s): 2

Explanation:

Routing decisions must be processed by the router, which relies on the networking device's CPU.

QUESTION 51:

A network technician needs to set up two public-facing web servers and wants to ensure that if they are compromised, the intruder cannot access the company's intranet. Which of the following methods should the technician use?

1. Place them behind a honeypot
2. Place them in a separate subnet
3. Place them between two identical firewalls
4. Place them in the demilitarized zone

Correct Answer(s): 4

Explanation:

A demilitarized zone (DMZ) is a sub-network inside a network and acts as a semi-trusted zone. It is used for servers that need to be public-facing, such as web, mail, FTP, and VoIP servers. The DMZ is treated as an untrusted zone by both the internet (public) and the intranet (private) zones.

QUESTION 52:

A network administrator has determined that the ingress and egress traffic of a router's interface are not being correctly reported to the monitoring server. Which of the following can be used to determine if the router interface uses 64b vs 32b counters?

1. SNMP walk
2. Packet analyzer
3. Syslog server
4. Port Scanner

Correct Answer(s): 1

Explanation:

SNMPWalk can be used to determine if the counter is using 32 bits or 64 bits by querying the OID of the endpoint (router interface). This is a complex topic that is actually beyond the scope of the Network+ exam (how to use SNMPWalk), and usually serves as a type of in-depth question that CompTIA might ask to determine if a candidate has actual real-world experience in networking or just studied from a textbook. Some instructors like to claim that CompTIA uses these types of questions to determine if someone is cheating, because only people who studied from a "brain dump" are likely to get this question correct! The reason you are seeing this type of question is to remind you that it is ok if you don't know all the answers on test day. Just take your best guess, and then move on!

QUESTION 53:

You are troubleshooting a recently installed NIC on a workstation and decided to ping the NIC's loopback address. Which of the following IPv4 addresses should you ping?

1. 10.0.0.1
2. 127.0.0.1
3. 172.16.1.1
4. 192.168.1.1

Correct Answer(s): 2

Explanation:

The loopback address is 127.0.0.1 in IPv4, and it is reserved for troubleshooting and testing. The loopback address is used to receive a test signal to the NIC and its software/drivers in order to diagnose problems. Even if the network cable is unplugged, you should be able to successfully ping your loopback address.

QUESTION 54:

A user is receiving certificate errors in other languages in their web browser when trying to access the company's main intranet site. Which of the following is the MOST likely cause of the issue?

1. DoS
2. Reflective DNS
3. Man-in-the-middle
4. ARP poisoning

Correct Answer(s): 3

Explanation:

A man-in-the-middle attack is a general term for when a perpetrator positions himself in a conversation between a user and an application, either to eavesdrop or to

impersonate one of the parties, making it appear as if a normal exchange of
information is occurring.

QUESTION 55:

Which of the following is a DNS record type?

1. TTL
2. DHCP
3. PTR
4. LDAP

Correct Answer(s): 3

Explanation:

There are several types of DNS records, including A, AAAA, CNAME, PTR, SVR,
and TXT. PTR records are used for the Reverse DNS (Domain Name System)
lookup. Using the IP address you can get the associated domain/hostname. An A
record should exist for every PTR record.

QUESTION 56:

Michael is a system administrator who is troubleshooting an issue with remotely
accessing a new server on the local area network. He is using an LMHOST file,
which contains the hostname and IP address of the new server. The server that he
cannot remotely access to is located on the same LAN as another server that he can
successfully remote to. What output from the command line would BEST resolve the
issue?

1. C:\windows\system32> ipconfig /flushdns Windows IP configuration
   Successfully flushed DNS resolver cache
2. C:\windows\system32> ipconfig /registerdns Windows IP
   configuration Registration of the DNS resource records for all adapters
   has been initiated. Any errors will be reported in the event viewer in 15
   minutes.
3. C:\windows\system32> nslookup Default server: unknownAddress:
   2.2.2.2
4. C:\windows\system32> nbtstat –R Successful purge and reload of the
   NBT remote cache table

Correct Answer(s): 4

Explanation:

Since he is using a local LMHOST file, it is bypassing the DNS of the machine, and flushing the DNS will not solve the problem. In this case, purging the contents of the NetBIOS name cache and then reloads the #PRE-tagged entries from the Lmhosts file.

QUESTION 57:

Which attack utilizes a wireless access point which has been made to look as if it belongs to the network in order to eavesdrop on the wireless traffic?

1.   Evil twin
2.   Rogue access point
3.   WEP attack
4.   War driving

Correct Answer(s): 1

Explanation:

An Evil Twin is meant to mimic a legitimate hotspot provided by a nearby business, such as a coffee shop that provides free Wi-Fi access to its patrons.

QUESTION 58:

You have been asked to troubleshoot a router which uses label-switching and label-edge routers to forward traffic. Which of the following types of protocols should you be familiar with in order to troubleshoot this device?

1.   BGP
2.   OSPF
3.   IS-IS
4.   MPLS

Correct Answer(s): 4

Explanation:

Multi-protocol label switching (MPLS) is a mechanism used within computer network infrastructures to speed up the time it takes a data packet to flow from one node to another. The label-based switching mechanism enables the network packets to flow on any protocol.

QUESTION 59:

What is the BEST way to secure the most vulnerable attack vector for a network?

1. Update all antivirus definitions on workstations and servers
2. Use biometrics and SSO for authentication
3. Remove unneeded services running on the servers
4. Provide end-user awareness training for office staff

Correct Answer(s): 4

Explanation:

Users are our most vulnerable attack vector, proper training can help reduce the risk.

QUESTION 60:

Which protocol is used to encapsulate other network layer protocols such as multicast and IPX over WAN connections?

1. MPLS
2. ESP
3. GRE
4. PPP

Correct Answer(s): 3

Explanation:

Generic Routing Encapsulation (GRE) is a protocol that encapsulates packets in order to route other protocols over IP networks.

QUESTION 61:

Which of the following BEST describes the process of documenting everyone who has physical access or possession of evidence?

1. Legal hold
2. Chain of custody
3. Secure copy protocol
4. Financial responsibility

Correct Answer(s): 2

Explanation:

Chain of custody refers to documentation that identifies all changes in the control, handling, possession, ownership, or custody of a piece of evidence.

QUESTION 62:

Johnny is trying to download a file from a remote FTP server, but keeps receiving an error that a connection cannot be opened. Which of the following should you do FIRST to resolve the problem?

1. Ensure that port 20 is open
2. Ensure that port 161 is open
3. Flush the DNS cache on the local workstation
4. Validate the security certificate from the host

Correct Answer(s): 1

Explanation:

Executing an FTP port connection through a client is a two-stage process requiring the use of two different ports. Once the user enters the name of the server and the login credentials in the authorization fields of the FTP client, the FTP connection is attempted over port 20. For FTP to function properly, you should have both ports 20 and 21 open.

QUESTION 63:

A user was moved from one cubicle in the office to a new one a few desks over. Now, they are reporting that their VoIP phone is randomly rebooting. When the network technician takes the VoIP phone and reconnects it in the old cubicle, it works without any issues. What is the cause of the problem?

1. Attenuation
2. Bad UPS
3. Cable short
4. Misconfigured DNS

Correct Answer(s): 3

Explanation:

Since the VoIP phone works in one cubicle but not another one that is very close, it is likely the new cubicle has a short in the cable running to the network jack or from

the jack to the VoIP phone. The network technician should test the new cubicle's
network jack to ensure there isn't an issue with the wiring.

QUESTION 64:

You are working as a forensic investigator for the police. The police have a search
warrant to capture a suspect's workstation as evidence for an ongoing criminal
investigation. As you enter the room with the policeman, he arrests the suspect and
handcuffs him. What should you do FIRST?

1. Turn off the workstation
2. Document the scene
3. Implement the chain of custody
4. Secure the area

Correct Answer(s): 4

Explanation:

As a forensic investigator, you should always 'secure the area' before you take any
other actions. This includes ensuring that no other people are in the area to disrupt
your forensic collection (such as the suspect or their accomplices), ensuring the
workstation isn't unplugged from the network or the power, and other actions to
prevent the evidence from being tampered with.

QUESTION 65:

Dion Training Solutions wants to migrate their email server from an on-premise
solution to a vendor-hosted web-based solution like G Suite or Gmail. Which of the
following types of cloud models best describes this proposed solution?

1. IaaS
2. PaaS
3. SaaS
4. SAN

Correct Answer(s): 3

Explanation:

Software as a Service (SaaS) uses the web to deliver applications that are managed by
a third-party vendor and whose interface is accessed on the client's side. Most SaaS
applications can be run directly from a web browser without any downloads or
installations required, although some require plugins. The G Suite and Gmail
solutions for business are a good example of a SaaS solution.

QUESTION 66:

When troubleshooting a T1 connection, the service provider's technical support representative instructs a network technician to place a special device into the CSU/DSU. Using this device, the provider is able to verify that communications are reaching the CSU/DSU. What was used by the network technician?

1. Cable analyzer
2. Toner probe
3. OTDR
4. Loopback plug

Correct Answer(s): 4

Explanation:

A loopback plug, also known as a loopback adaptor or a loopback cable, is a device used to test ports (such as serial, parallel, USB, and network ports) to identify network and network interface card (NIC) issues. Loopback plug equipment facilitates the testing of simple networking issues and is available at very low costs.

QUESTION 67:

You are trying to select the BEST network topology for a new network based on the following requirements. The design must include redundancy using a minimum of two cables to create the network. The network should not be prone to congestion, therefore each device must wait for its turn to communicate on the network by passing around a token. Which of the following topologies would BEST meet the client's requirements?

1. Star
2. Bus
3. Mesh
4. Ring

Correct Answer(s): 4

Explanation:

A ring topology is a local area network (LAN) in which the nodes (workstations or other devices) are connected in a closed loop configuration. Ring topologies aren't used heavily in local area networks anymore, but they are still commonly found in wide area network connections as a FDDI ring. A FDDI ring is a Fiber Distributed Data Interface ring, which allows for a network that can communicate up to 120 miles in range, uses a ring-based token network as its basis, and uses two counter-rotating token ring topologies to comprise the single network. This provides redundancy for the network because if one cable is broken or fails, the other can maintain the network operations. The token is used to control which device can communicate on the network, preventing any congestion or collisions.

QUESTION 68:

While monitoring the network, you notice that the network traffic to one of the servers is extremely high. Which of the following should you utilize to verify if this is a concern?

1. Log management
2. Network diagram
3. Network baseline
4. Real-time monitor

Correct Answer(s): 3

Explanation:

High network traffic can be a sign of a possible attack conducted either by an insider or someone out of the network to steal relevant information. By reviewing the network baseline, you can determine if the traffic is actually high and if any configurations of the network are out of baseline causing the issue. By knowing what "normal" looks like, you can then more easily identify the abnormal.

QUESTION 69:

A small office has an Internet connection that drops out at least two times per week. It often takes until the next day for the service provider to come out and fix the issue. What should you create with the service provider to reduce this downtime in the future?

1. NDA
2. SLA
3. SOW
4. MOU

Correct Answer(s): 2

Explanation:

A service level agreement (SLA) is a contract between a service provider (either internal or external) and the end user that defines the level of service expected from the service provider. SLAs are output-based that their purpose is specifically to define what the customer will receive. If the customer requires faster response times, it should be in the SLA.

QUESTION 70:

You are performing a high-availability test of a system. As part of the test, you create an interruption on the fiber connection to the network, but the network traffic was not re-routed automatically. Which type of routing is the system utilizing?

1. Static
2. Dynamic
3. Hybrid
4. Loop

Correct Answer(s): 1

Explanation:

Static routes must be configured and re-routed manually during an issue. Dynamic and Hybrid would reroute automatically during a network interruption.

QUESTION 71:

A technician receives a report that a user's workstation is experiencing no network connectivity. The technician investigates and notices the patch cable running from the back of the user's VoIP phone is routed directly under the rolling chair and has been repeatedly smashed. What is the likely cause of the problem?

1. Cross-talk
2. Cable was not properly crimped
3. Excessive collisions
4. Split pairs

Correct Answer(s): 1

Explanation:

Cross-talk and EMI occur when signals experience interference. Since the cable has been repeatedly run over, its shielding could be damaged since the cable is no longer made up of the same consistency and cross-talk could occur between the pairs.

QUESTION 72:

You want to install a perimeter device on the network that will help ensure FTP commands are not being sent out over port 25. Which of the following devices would allow for deep packet inspection to catch this type of activity?

1. Layer 7 firewall
2. Web proxy

3. Layer 3 switch
4. Protocol analyzer

Correct Answer(s): 1

Explanation:

Layer 7 firewalls are application-filtering firewalls. FTP traffic does not usually travel over port 25, and should travel over port 21. By using a Layer 7 firewall, the device can perform a deep packet inspection (DPI) to identify which application or protocol is actually being used to send traffic over a given port.

QUESTION 73:

Andy is a network technician who is preparing to configure a company's network. He has installed a firewall to allow for an internal DMZ and an external network. No hosts on the internal network should be directly accessible by their IP address from the Internet, but they should be able to reach remote networks if they have been assigned an IP address within the network. Which of the following IP addressing solutions would work for this particular network configuration?

1. Teredo tunneling
2. Private
3. APIPA
4. Classless

Correct Answer(s): 2

Explanation:

A private IP address is an IP address that's reserved for internal use behind a router or other Network Address Translation (NAT) devices, apart from the public. Private IP addresses provide an entirely separate set of addresses that still allow access on a network but without taking up a public IP address space.

QUESTION 74:

Which of the following is the BEST way to prevent different types of security threats from occurring within your network on a regular basis?

1. Disaster recovery planning
2. User training and awareness
3. Penetration testing
4. Business continuity training

Correct Answer(s): 2

Explanation:

Users are the biggest vulnerability on your network. Therefore, increasing user training can decrease the number of security threats that are realized on your networks. According to industry best practices, you should conduct end user security awareness training at least annually (if not more frequently).

QUESTION 75:

A network technician just finished configuring a new interface on a router, but the client workstations are not receiving the addressing information from the new interface. Which of the following should be added or changed to allow the workstations to connect to the new interface?

1. TTL
2. MX record
3. IP helper
4. DHCP lease time

Correct Answer(s): 3

Explanation:

DHCP IP Helper addresses enable a single DHCP server to provide DHCP IP addresses to every PC on the network, regardless of whether they are on the same broadcast domain as the DHCP server or not. DHCP IP Helper addresses are IP addresses configured on a routed interface such as a VLAN Interface or a routers Ethernet interface that allows that specific device to act as a "middle man" which forwards BOOTP (Broadcast) DHCP request it receives on an interface to the DHCP server specified by the IP Helper address via unicast. By adding an IP Helper address to the new interface on the router, it will allow the DHCP broadcast requests to be forwarded to the workstations.